Green Ivy Publishing
1 Lincoln Centre
18W140 Butterfield Road
Suite 1500
Oakbrook Terrace IL 60181-4843
www.greenivybooks.com

ISBN: 978-1-944680-09-1

"A lasting imprint of the words from the Hippocratic oath, still recited at many medical school graduations is 'do no harm.' Too bad that oath is not required of the resources that pay for the services of those required to 'do no harm.' Leslie Boyd has painted a picture of distress and a plea for justice as she emphatically calls on all of us to heed the message of her son's life—and death—and acknowledge that our medical care reimbursement is also vulnerable to the whims of those not yet guided by that centuries old demand: 'Do NO Harm!'"

— Olson Huff, MD FAAP, *The Sixty-Second Parent*

"This is the compelling and eloquent story of a tenacious mother who relished and fought for her son's life, endured his tragic death, and turned that tragedy into a heroic fight for health care for all. An inspiration for all who hope to stand up for our common humanity."

— Timothy B. Tyson, Duke University, *Blood Done Sign My Name*

"Leslie Boyd has shown an unyielding commitment to justice and care for all people. Her story inspires and calls you embrace your own cause with relentless commitment."

— Rev. Dr. William J. Barber II, president NC NAACP

Life o' Mike

A Memoir by Leslie Boyd

For Daddy, whose love for me was unconditional.

And for Mike who lives forever in my heart, and whose wicked sense of humor still makes me laugh at the most inappropriate things.

Life o' Mike

The short, wild, incredibly awesome life of a jackass

Introduction

When Michael was born, I began to keep a diary. I wanted him to know when he grew up why I made the decisions I made when he was an infant. I wanted him to know I loved him from the start, as much as if he had been healthy like his big brother was.

I wrote more in those diaries than just his story because Michael's life affected mine. Like many parents of children with birth defects and other medical problems, his father and I had different ways of dealing with the hurt of having an ill child. I was determined to be stoic; he saw me as cold. He was visibly hurt; I saw him as weak. Of course, neither of us was right. I tucked my pain away in my diaries and he worked, sometimes twelve hours a day, seven days a week. We drifted apart until nothing, not even our children, could draw us back together.

I hadn't read those diaries in a dozen or more years, until Michael once again faced a crisis that ultimately would take his life.

I believed that if I loved him enough, it would compensate for the pain of being born with a less than perfect body. He would draw strength from my love and everything would be fine, just like the articles I read in Christian magazines growing up. My love, together with God's, would suffice.

Of course, that wasn't God's plan at all. Michael would face several surgeries, a learning disability, and unpopularity because of his physical problems. As a teenager, he would turn to drugs and alcohol, and later, to a disastrous marriage, to ease his pain.

He sobered up at age twenty-two, and like any recovering addict, he was never home free; he just coped with each day.

Looking back at the diaries, I marvel at how little I knew, how even though I thought my naiveté had been shattered in the recovery room, I was wrong. I was naive about so many things.

Through it all, I drew strength from the belief that tomorrow would be better, but many days it wasn't.

Today I know that tomorrow may not be better, but there is hope. His life was a blessing to me and to everyone who loved him, and in his memory, we fight for access to health care for every American.

The sound of his heart filled his ears.

He'd fix that soon.

He stopped in the middle of the bridge and looked down.

About thirty feet, he figured. Good. Below him was a concrete ledge jutting out maybe ten feet above the water.

He could almost hear his body thud against it and he wondered if that was what would kill him.

Maybe it would just knock him unconscious so he wouldn't panic when the murky water filled his lungs and carried him off to peace.

Twenty-two, and all I've done is fail. Just a huge disappointment to everybody who ever loved me. My friends are getting sick of hearing about it.

Mom keeps hoping, and I keep letting her down. I can't believe she still thinks I'll do something with my life. I don't know if it's optimism or blind stupidity. Rob hasn't convinced her yet that I'm useless. I'm not going anywhere.

And Dad, Jesus, Dad. Does he even have a clue? He's so wrapped up in his life with Linda and Scott. I don't think he even thinks about me except to wish I'd disappear.

G, she'll just be happy to hear I'm gone. Maybe nobody will tell her. She'll call one day and Mom will say, "Didn't you hear? He's dead. You killed him." Mom will blame her. She can't believe it's all my fault and she can't fix it. She always thinks she can fix it.

Bobsey's out looking for me. He knows. I drank way more than usual tonight. The hard stuff, too. I probably pissed him off but good. God, I'm a lousy drunk. You'd think by now I'd be good at it. I've been doing it long enough.

His heart was still pounding as he leaned over the rail.

A little more . . . a little more and it'll all be over. They'll find me in the morning somewhere downstream. Maybe I'll float all the way out to the Hudson before they find me.

Chapter 1

Sometimes after school, Narda Rockhill and I would go to her house. Her baby brother would be in the kitchen, propped in his high chair, grinning, giggling, and reaching for us. That was about all he could do, and there was little hope he would ever do much more.

Narda and I played with him, handing him a ball and retrieving it when he dropped it—his version of catch.

None of us loved him any less because of his limitations. In fact, the whole family loved him more. It was easy to love him because loving the people around him was the thing he did best.

But then, I could go home. I didn't have to worry about who would care for him when he got too big to carry around, or when I got too old and frail, or if he outlived me.

I didn't know how Narda's mother did it. I wondered if she cried herself to sleep at night or if she lay awake and prayed for strength.

I knew I would never be able to cope with a less than perfect child.

"God would never give you a burden you couldn't bear," the women at church always said when something terrible happened to someone else. That's what they said when the mother of three young children died of cancer and her husband was left grief-stricken, but with no time to grieve. That's what they said about the missionary's wife whose premature infant died in Borneo, and whose next child was born prematurely and diagnosed a few months later with severe cerebral palsy. She would never walk or speak.

Those people coped, but I knew I couldn't. So God would give me only perfect children.

#

Danny was perfect. Big, solid, football player material like his Uncle Fred. My second son would be the same way.

Barbara Powell, my obstetrician, remarked all through my pregnancy how strong his heartbeat was, and he was active. Really active, bruised my ribs from the inside.

I knew it was a boy although Dr. Powell kept calling him she. I even predicted he would be born November 3rd, my twenty-second birthday. Like any expectant mother, all my plans were for a healthy baby.

That was the only thing I got wrong.

I contracted a rare virus when I was about six weeks pregnant. It was called pityriasis rosea, and its effect on developing embryos had never been studied, but we did know it was related to rubella—German measles. Dr. Powell thought it would be best if I had an abortion and tried again. I refused. This was my baby and I wouldn't love him any less if he had problems. I still believed God wouldn't give me any burden I couldn't bear; I just didn't know how much I could bear.

Except for the constant backache, my pregnancy was uneventful. The baby never seemed to sleep, but I didn't mind the movement. Danny hardly ever moved. I had to poke him a couple of times a day to get him to move at all, and he was a great sleeper as an infant. I knew that would be unlikely with this one.

Dr. Powell was out of town the weekend Michael was born. I woke up in labor at 5:30 on that Sunday morning and called her partner, a woman who didn't particularly want a sentient patient in the delivery room with her.

In Georgia in 1974, mothers routinely got knocked out when delivering. Dr. Powell hadn't been too keen on having me stay awake for the delivery.

Doctors—even women doctors—were paternalistic. When I first met her, Dr. Powell asked whether I preferred to be called Leslie or if I had a nickname.

I told her Leslie would be fine and asked if she was a Barbara, Barbie or Barb.

She looked insulted. "I am *Doctor* Powell," she snapped.

"Then I'm Mrs. Danforth," I replied.

I had gone to general practitioners all my life, most of whom weren't quite so full of themselves. The doctor who delivered Danny was an old country doctor, full of common sense and respect for his patients.

When Danny didn't seem to want baby food, he told me the stuff was full of salt anyway, and I should just puree whatever we were eating. If Danny seemed to react to any food, we'd take him off it. When I asked whether he recommended breast feeding, he replied, "Cow's milk is for baby cows."

But that was in semirural Wisconsin. In Augusta, Georgia, the attitude was different.

"When you go into labor, we'll get you into the hospital and give you something to put you to sleep and when you wake up you'll have a brand new baby," Dr. Powell had said when I was three months pregnant. I set her straight. I was going to be there to welcome my child into the world. End of discussion.

"But what if you need a caesarean?" she asked.

"I'll have a spinal," I replied. "You do not have my permission to knock me out. Period."

It was easier for the doctor if the mother was deadweight. It was easier for the mother if she felt no pain. That was their thinking. Mine was that I had carried this child for nine months, lost sleep, felt bloated and ungainly, and been bruised from the inside. I was going to be among the first to see him.

When I called Dr. Powell's partner, she knew who I was.

"Oh," she said with a decided lack of enthusiasm. "You're the one who wants to stay awake."

I had never met the woman. I would never see her again. I do remember her name—Carol Pryor. But she knew me; I was the troublemaker.

When I was seven months pregnant, I had sat in Dr. Powell's waiting room for three hours before I went to the window to ask what the delay was about.

"Oh, Doctor is delivering a baby," the receptionist chirped.

"Well, Doctor has missed her appointment with me," I said. "Why were none of us told so we could reschedule? Does Doctor have so little respect for us that she thinks our time has no value?"

I left without seeing the doctor and a few days later I got a bill for a missed appointment because I hadn't canceled twenty-four hours in advance of my appointment. I went to the typewriter and made up my own bill.

She was charging me $45 for the missed appointment, so I charged her $45 for the three hours of my time that I had wasted when she missed her appointment with me. I never got another bill for that missed appointment.

Nowadays, I allow a half hour or so before I go to the window and announce that the doctor has missed his or her appointment with me and we'll have to reschedule.

Carol knew all about me, and I'm sure she was not happy at having to care for me, especially since I would be awake.

The nurses in the labor and delivery department ran interference for me.

"Excuse us, Doctor, we're a little busy right now," they said if the doctor tried to talk to me during a contraction.

Michael Timothy Danforth was born at 8:30 a.m., November 3, 1974. I had been in labor just three hours. I like to say that it was the only time Michael was ever easy.

"This baby gets a ten on his Apgar," the doctor said.

Good, I thought. He's perfect. He was healthy, screaming.

The nurses wrapped him quickly and handed him to me.

"Don't unwrap him," they cautioned. "Remember, he's just come from a ninety-eight-point-six room into a seventy-two-degree one."

He quieted as soon as he was in my arms. He was blonde, blue-eyed and so wide awake, much more delicate than his brother, a full pound lighter, smaller-boned. Over my protests, they whisked him off to the nursery as they wheeled me into recovery.

"Doctor has to take a look at him," the nurse said. "We'll bring him to you soon."

I figured they didn't know what to do with a mother who was wide awake. Here I was, alert and wanting my baby. Highly irregular. Highly inconvenient.

They left me alone in recovery, a room with two beds and a curtain between them. The woman in the next bed was sobbing.

"Are you OK?" I asked.

"I don't know," she said. "They're trying to stop my labor. I'm only six months pregnant. I don't know how to make the contractions stop."

Six months. My best friend had lost a set of twin boys in her sixth month.

I'll say a prayer for you," I said.

"How about you?" she asked.

"A boy," I said. "Healthy, thank God."

I rolled over to rest. She tried not to cry. I heard someone paging Matthew Howard, my pediatrician, but I didn't think anything of it until he walked into the room holding Michael and accompanied by two nurses and Hazen.

"Something's wrong!" I said. I held my breath hoping someone would laugh at my new mother's nerves. No one did.

"We have a problem," Dr. Howard said.

That moment is etched in my memory because it marks the moment my naiveté first was shattered. There is the *before that moment,* when nothing that bad would ever happen to me, and then there's *post-moment,* when I knew nothing was more important than getting the best help available for my child.

I knew when Matt Howard defined Michael's birth defect as "our" problem that he was invested fully in caring for Michael. I didn't want a doctor who would describe the problem as "his" or "yours."

"He has a pretty rare condition called exstrophy of the bladder. His bladder is inside-out on his abdomen, and he has a split along the top of his penis, called epispadius."

The obstetrician had called in a specialist, a urologist, who would examine Michael and then come talk to me.

Dr. Blanchard was an old-fashioned, I-know-best doctor. He didn't have to tell me the whole story because he was the doctor and I wasn't.

"He'll be fine," Dr. Blanchard told me. "We'll just close up the bladder and he'll be fine."

So it wasn't all that serious after all, I thought. Just a matter of some minor surgery and he'll be as normal as anyone.

I had told the nurses it was my birthday, so they told the kitchen, and I got black walnut cake with walnut frosting with my lunch.

I hate black walnut cake. I'm not wild about walnuts at all. I took one look and started to cry. It wasn't about Michael; it was about having to eat cake I didn't like to celebrate my birthday. Really.

\#

As one of five children, I saw my birthday as my own personal national holiday. I still do.

Michael's and my shared birthday would be the source of jokes all his life.

"It's really my birthday," I would tell him as I handed him his gifts. "I had it first."

"I have it better," he replied.

"You can have it when I'm done with it," I said.

Every November 3, we got up and sang "Happy birthday to ME" to each other as loudly as we could. It was tradition before he was ten. When he moved out, we sang it over the telephone.

When a friend's wife had a baby boy on her birthday, the friend called to deliver the news and Michael scrambled to pick up the extension phone.

"You can tell that poor kid right now he's never going to have a party on HIS birthday because Mom doesn't want a dozen screaming kids in the house on HER birthday!" he said, and hung up.

"Sounds like somebody has issues," my friend said.

"Nah, he's fine," I replied.

Meanwhile, Mike was standing behind me, laughing, hoping my friend was shocked at his outburst.

Birthdays are special in my family, and Mike and I loved to pretend we hated sharing ours, and we competed for attention and favors.

#

The day he was born, all I wanted was a hot fudge sundae. Hazen refused to go out to get one until the nurse shamed him into it. On his way out, he made a phone call to his boss to say he was taking a few days off.

"I told him about the baby's birth defect," he said as he handed me the ice cream.

Birth defect.

I hadn't thought of it in that term.

Birth defect.

Imperfection.

Defective.

That's not how I thought of Michael. He was perfect, except for his bladder and penis. This wasn't a *real* birth defect like spina bifida or the flipper limbs the thalidomide babies had. This wasn't like Narda's little brother or the missionary's daughter. If this was really bad I'd never be able to cope and I was coping fine. Birth defect sounded overly dramatic, like an exaggeration of what was real.

The fact that Michael's problem was going to be easy to fix meant he was very nearly perfect and still a miracle in my eyes.

Matt Howard came back at five o'clock.

"I've been in the med school library all afternoon," he said.

He had studied up on exstrophy, and he offered to let his partner, a more experienced pediatrician, take the case.

I figured anybody who was willing to spend a Sunday afternoon studying was dedicated enough for me.

"They're wringing out diapers like mad in the nursery," he said. "So, we're past the first hurdle—his kidneys are working."

"Huh?"

"Well, sometimes, children with this—well, sometimes their kidneys don't work."

I grilled him on what else I might expect.

Dr. Blanchard had lied to me. The prognosis was good, once it was established that his kidneys worked.

But his bladder wasn't going to work, and he could develop kidney problems. I was furious. How could a doctor—someone I needed to be able to trust—lie to me?

Matt asked if I wanted him to be there when Dr. Blanchard came in the next morning.

"That's OK," I said. "I can fire him by myself."

That's what I did. He came into the room all smiles and asked how Mommy was doing and I confronted him about his lies.

The bladder couldn't just be closed up because the sphincter muscle wouldn't work. The prognosis was OK, now that we knew his kidneys were working. But he could have been in serious condition—and I wasn't told.

"Well," he said in defense of his actions, "you just had a baby and I didn't want to worry you."

Right. And that baby had serious problems and since I was the one who was going to make the decisions about his care, I was going to be informed and involved.

Blanchard was shocked. He was the expert; I was just a mother. Rather than apologize for his paternalistic attitude, he defended it and was more than a little put out by my attempt to interfere in his plan for Michael's care.

"I can't trust anything you tell me now," I said. "I'm afraid you're fired. Please stay out of the nursery and away from him."

Barbara Powell and Hazen were both shocked that I would fire someone who knew more about Michael's condition than I did. But Matt supported me. He promised to help me find a specialist who would respect me and work with me.

Matt also ordered the nurses to bring him to me for feedings. They wanted to supplement his feedings with bottles so I could get rest, and they only wanted to bring him to me once every four hours during the day. So my reputation as a troublemaker was solidified.

Hazen always took a *they-know-best* attitude; I rejected it completely. I leaned toward the *question-authority* end of the scale. I have always leaned that way.

As the daughter of a newspaper reporter, I questioned everything, and I wanted to know the answers. Doctors in the Deep South in 1974 didn't like to be questioned. I needed to find the rare specialists who would accept me as a partner in my son's care.

The first night in my room, another woman was brought in. She was six months pregnant after trying for two years, and her baby had just died in the womb. No one knew why—it just happened. The orderlies came in the morning and took her away to knock her out and induce labor so she wouldn't have to see her dead baby—as though her feelings would disappear with the corpse, as though she would be better off never seeing her child.

In those not so distant days, women were told to get over it and try again, as though the baby they had been carrying wasn't real. Women's grief was dismissed as over-emotionalism. For most of us, the chair is at the table and the place is set as soon as we know there's a baby on the way. Years later, when I would write about support groups and memorial services for parents who had lost babies, many, many older women told me they had lost babies thirty or more years before and that this was the first time they felt they had permission to grieve.

I knew a lot about each of my children before they were born. I thought of them by the names we had chosen, not as "it."

My baby was less than perfect, but he was strong and would lead a normal life. I had much to be grateful for.

The day before we went home, Diane Kahres came in to have her sixth baby. She was being induced, so we spent much of the night talking.

Diane would become one of my pillars of strength in the years ahead. I don't know whether I would have been able to hold it all together if she hadn't been there to listen and advise me and to look after Danny when it wasn't appropriate for him to be with us. She understood his toddler babbling and was kind and patient. She understood "fuppin to grick" meant "something to drink," even when Hazen didn't. She understood toddler-speak, and she understood how life could throw curveballs. Nothing rattled her, and she gave me the confidence to keep moving on days I had grown weary of having to make decisions that I barely understood.

One more kid never bothered Diane.

"Once you have four, another one or two hardly matters," she said. "The bigger ones help look after the little ones. It's easy."

Chapter 2

Hazen's father, known affectionately as Chief, was already at the apartment when we brought Michael home. In fact, by the time I got home in the early afternoon, little Danny had already downed a half dozen cans of Pepsi and a canister of Pringles. Hazen's mother, Laura, arrived the next day and promptly rearranged the kitchen.

Danny was wired, and Michael was wide awake, seemingly soaking everything in. He stayed awake all afternoon, not fussing, just taking in all the sounds around him, and we all marveled at how alert he was.

Hazen's brother, Fred, came two days after I got home, and our little two-bedroom apartment was bursting. We had to rent cots for Laura and Grampie Danny, who slept in the living room. During the day, we folded the cots and rolled them into a corner in the dining room.

Michael was less than a week old when Laura's friend, Ruby Pike, dropped by. She lived an hour away and was eager to see her old friend. We spent the evening hearing Ruby drone on about a recent heart attack as I rocked Michael. He was content to be awake in my arms. I wanted to be asleep.

". . . And I was sure I would die. There I was on the gurney . . ." She began to sound like the teacher in the Peanuts cartoons: "Whaaaaah *waaaaahh* whaaaaah."

I rocked in time to the cadence of her words and struggled to stay awake. I was the hostess, after all.

The next day, Danny ate a mushroom growing under the pine trees in the yard, and Hazen panicked.

Hazen always did expect the worst. He worried even when things were going well because something was sure to go wrong.

I called the poison-control center and they said there were no harmful mushrooms growing in the area in November, but Hazen had already run out to get syrup of ipecac to induce vomiting.

"We don't need to do this," I said.

"We can't take chances," he said as he poured a couple teaspoons down the child's throat. "The poison control center could be wrong."

After someone takes syrup of ipecac, they have to drink water until they vomit. Danny, barely two, didn't want to drink the water, but Hazen kept working on it until Danny threw up.

Thinking that was the end of it, he and Fred gave Danny a Snickers bar as a reward for cooperating.

Turns out you should wait a couple hours after taking syrup of ipecac before eating a Snickers bar. I refused to clean up the mess.

As much as Danny was a great sleeper as a baby, Michael was great at being awake. He was happy as long as he could see what was going on around him, so he spent hours in the baby swing, entertained by Danny playing or me doing housework. He loved being held. Danny had wanted his independence, even as an infant, but Michael was a cuddler.

Michael was about ten days old when Dave Skeel called. Dave was a urologist on staff at the Medical College of Georgia in Augusta.

"I talked to Matt Howard and I thought you might have questions," he said after introducing himself. "You don't have to hire me, but I can answer any questions you have. I know the whole thing must be overwhelming."

I hired him.

At three weeks, Michael had an appointment with Matt Howard, and Matt gave me the rest of the news: Michael had an orthopedic problem. His pelvic bone was split and rotated back, so he likely wouldn't walk before he had surgery to correct it. The defect is common among children with exstrophy. He also had inguinal hernias on both sides of his groin – also common among children with exstrophy.

"How could you not tell me about this in the hospital?" I asked. "What else is wrong? What else are you keeping from me?"

Matt hadn't been sure about the hernias when Michael was in the hospital, and he wasn't certain the pelvic bone defect was serious enough to require surgery. He apologized again and again for not telling me right away about it.

That was the way doctors dealt with patients. Don't tell them everything at once. Let them absorb things a little at a time.

But it left me in a panic. I didn't believe there was nothing else wrong. Would he have other problems? Were his heart and lungs OK? What about his brain? It took Matt and Dave weeks to convince me I knew everything there was to know. Matt promised he would never withhold information from me again, and he kept his word. He and Dave both answered questions, offered me reading material, and informed me about any new developments in treatment.

Michael was almost three months old when I volunteered for the Mother's March Against Birth Defects, a March of Dimes fundraiser. I went door-to-door in the apartment complex—106 apartments—with Michael in my arms. The complex, which was one of the closest to the army base, Fort Gordon, never raised a whole lot for any cause. People moved in and out pretty quickly, and most didn't become involved in the community.

But a lot of people knew I had a baby who had a birth defect, and when I showed up at the door, they gave. I set the record for money raised in that apartment complex.

As an adult, Michael would call that "playing the sick kid card."

Michael hated doctors, but he loved Dave, and the feeling was mutual. I knew I could call Matt or Dave any time of the day with any question, no matter how trivial, and both of them proved to be effective at intervening in the bureaucracy of medical care when I needed them.

When Michael had his first kidney X-ray, the radiologist told me not to feed him for an hour before the test. I sat in the waiting room for an hour, two hours, three hours . . . Michael was howling, and the radiologist said it would be another hour or so and I still shouldn't feed him. I fed him, rebel that I was. There was no need for him to suffer if it was going to be another hour, and it was.

He was gaining weight slowly, and I was paranoid about him missing meals. He couldn't have surgery until he was twenty pounds, and unlike Danny, he didn't gain weight easily.

Finally, we were called into the X-ray room, where technicians poked him in both arms and both feet, trying to inject the dye that was needed for the test. Again and again they stuck him, refusing to call anyone from pediatrics to help find a vein that would work for the infusion.

I stood by as they poked and stuck him, up one arm and down the other, asking if there might be someone who could do this any better. They acted as though I wasn't there, and I stood by wondering whether they really knew how to work on a six-week-old infant.

After he was bruised up and down both arms and on his feet, someone suggested they look for a vein in his head.

That was my breaking point.

I picked him up and walked out of the room. I looked for a telephone and called Dave's office. Within minutes, he was in the room, demanding someone call the pediatric department for help. I had an ally, and even in 1974, allies were necessary in health care.

I needed someone I could call on who would appear and demand the right thing be done, and I had it in Dave. I also had someone who would be honest with me and who was willing to engage me in conversation and in the necessary decisions about Michael's care.

Dave told me the same thing Matt had said—Michael's bladder wasn't going to work and it would have to be removed. But, he said, Michael wouldn't have to have a bag attached to his abdomen. There was a new procedure—bilateral ureterosigmoidostomy. Michael's ureters could be implanted into his sigmoid colon. It would be more difficult for him to control his bowels at first, but he wouldn't have any outward evidence of his birth defect except for a couple of surgical scars.

"There's an increased chance of benign tumors at the implant site, but the surgery can be reversed if that happens," he said. "It's about one in thirteen hundred."

The odds sounded good to me, and even though Dave was reluctant to make the decision right then, it was the one we finally agreed on as best for Michael. I wanted him to look and feel as normal as possible. I thought ahead to middle school gym class and thought how his peers might laugh at a urine bag on his belly, but they wouldn't see a bilateral uretero-sigmoidostomy.

We met Dr. Ed Berg, an orthopedist practicing at the Medical College of Georgia a few weeks later. Michael was going to need surgery to correct the pelvic bone defect. He wouldn't be able to walk before it was corrected because the way his legs currently rotated out would prevent him from balancing properly.

Or so Ed said.

Michael started pulling himself up on the furniture when he was seven months old and he stood bowlegged. He let go of the furniture and took off when he was a year.

I called Ed to ask whether it was OK for him to walk.

"Oh, he won't walk," Ed said.

"He's walking."

Ed asked me to bring Michael in. He was waiting with a movie camera to catch it all on film.

"I've never seen this," he said as Michael took off down the hospital corridor, a streak of red corduroy and white sneakers with blonde hair. I'm sure that footage was shown at more than one orthopedic conference.

Of course, Michael still would need surgery and Ed suggested the bladder and orthopedic surgery be done at one time. It would eliminate the added risk of another surgery, and I knew that every time you administer anesthesia, you run a risk.

I decided that would be the best course.

Chapter 3

The decisions were pretty much mine to make. I was the one who dealt with the doctors and the medical stuff; Hazen was the breadwinner. When Michael had doctors' appointments, I got up at 5:00 a.m., dragged the kids out of bed, and took Hazen to work so I could have the car. On those days that I was also assigned a number of errands: get the oil changed, have the air conditioner looked at, stop by the insurance agent's office, pick up groceries . . . by the end of the day, when I picked him up at work, I was done in, and so were the kids.

Hazen didn't trust anybody else to look after Michael—not even himself. I was to be with him all the time until he had surgery at about fifteen months. There were a couple of times we went out because office politics demanded we both be there, so we hired a nurse and stayed the shortest time we could get away with.

The first time we went out, we hired Mrs. Faircloth through an agency and she came with good recommendations. She loved children and was an RN, so she would be able to handle a medical emergency, even though it was no more likely with Michael than with any other child.

When we came home, I found her weeping over Michael. I took him from her and Hazen paid her.

I was furious. I didn't want people weeping over Michael; I wanted him to feel empowered, not sorry for himself. I wasn't going to cry over him and neither was anyone else. Mrs. Faircloth never looked after him again.

In my little world, courage and love would be enough to solve everything. I was going to be the strong mother who would make Michael's world OK.

It turned out I was a strong mother. I fought doctors, school systems, therapists and more when his needs weren't met. But love and courage wouldn't be enough to solve everything.

Hazen's world was his career. He worked to get ahead while I worked to raise the boys. For awhile, that was OK, but month after month after month, I was home while he—and the car—were at work. I could walk around the apartment complex and visit other stay-at-home moms, but that was as far as my world went most days. That was supposed to be enough for me.

Eventually, it wasn't. I couldn't get to a library or bookstore; there were no computers back then. The outside world consisted of Phil Donohue and the TV news. There wasn't even cable.

My family was eight hundred miles away, and I couldn't even talk to them without Hazen timing the conversation because long-distance calls cost money. I wrote tons of letters, but it wasn't the same as being there or hearing their voices.

I joke that depression doesn't just run in my family—it gallops. In 1975, we didn't have serotonin reuptake inhibitors. Depression was something that nobody talked about and nobody admitted to having.

As the months went by, I felt increasingly isolated and sad—and ashamed that I could feel that way when Danny was healthy, Michael's prognosis was good, and Hazen's career was going well.

I looked forward to the surgery, hoping I would feel a little less isolated after it was over.

#

Michael was supposed to have surgery before Christmas 1975, but he came down with the chicken pox, so we postponed it until February. Diane Kahres offered to take Danny during the day while Michael was in the hospital. Danny loved her and her family, and they doted on him. I knew I wouldn't have to worry about him, at least not until it was time for him to come home.

So, I concentrated on getting Michael ready. I tried to put weight on him every way I could imagine. He was fifteen months old and a mere nineteen pounds. He was likely going to lose weight just before the surgery because of the bowl-cleansing protocol. The nutrition he would be on would be mixed with Tang to give it a tolerable taste, and he would be allowed to drink it from a baby bottle, even though he was weaned. It would be months before we got him off the bottle again.

Mike liked the hospital to begin with. Dave visited him every day, and Matt stopped by most days. Ed Berg was busy designing an eight-pound brace that would do the same job as a forty-pound body cast.

Mike loved the nutrition regimen—he could run around the surgical and pediatric floors with bottle in hand, socializing with everyone. He gained two pounds.

We got to know many of the parents and children on the pediatrics unit. There's camaraderie among parents of children in the hospital. We all knew each child's story; we all had medical disaster stories; we looked out for each other's children. If a parent needed to get out to eat, another would sit with the child.

"He should nap until I'm back, but if he doesn't . . ."

"Don't worry about it. I'll play his favorite game with him."

When children were in surgery, parents sat together, comforting each other and preparing each other for post-op.

"She'll look like a hardware store when they wheel her in. I almost fainted the first time I saw it, but it's OK; it's just monitors and drainage tubes. It will all be gone in a couple days."

For the days of prep before Michael's surgery, all went well – until the antibiotics regimen started.

Michael was allergic to sulfa drugs, and the night before his surgery was scheduled, his fever spiked to 105 as I tried to get the nurses to stop giving him the medicine.

I stood next to his crib and threatened one nurse as she insisted his orders said he had to have it. She refused to call Dave to see if she could stop giving it, then sneaked into the room while I was in the bathroom and gave him another dose. He immediately threw it up, and I called Dave at home to get him to make them stop.

The nurse was written up, but I spent the night sponging Michael with cool water to try and get his fever down.

In the morning, an orderly came to get a urine sample.

"He doesn't urinate," I said. "It comes directly through the ureters into his diaper, drop by drop."

"Well," he said, "we could tie a bag round his little pee-pee and wait."

"We'd be waiting a long, long time," I said. "His urine doesn't come through his penis."

"Of course it does."

I finally had to take off Michael's diaper and show him, and then he wanted to tape a bag around the edge of Michael's bladder.

It wasn't until one of the nurses wandered in and told him to check with the doctor that he finally gave up.

It was about 7:00 a.m. when another orderly came in to take him to surgery. I tried to insist he talk to the doctor first because Michael still had a fever and he was weak from the reaction to the antibiotic.

He said he didn't need to talk to anyone and reached for the crib. I held on for dear life. I knew Michael was too weak to withstand eight hours of surgery and I believed if I let go, I wouldn't see Michael alive again.

Hazen reached over and pried my fingers off the crib, insisting that Dave wouldn't let Michael die, and the orderly took off running with me close behind. By the time I reached the elevator, the doors were just closing and Michael was crying hysterically.

Parents weren't allowed anywhere near the operating room then, so I went downstairs to the cafeteria for coffee.

An hour went by, and Dave came in.

"I have some bad news," he said, and I leapt to my feet, panic overwhelming me.

"They killed him!" I choked.

"Let me rephrase," he said. "We're going to reschedule the surgery for next week to give him time to recover. You didn't think I'd let anything happen to him, did you?"

I had thought they would anesthetize him before Dave got there and that would be the end.

Even now, I get the creeps when I see a child being wheeled into surgery – anybody's child. Even on TV. There's no feeling more helpless than that of turning over your child to someone else and not being able to do anything to change what's going to happen.

Chapter 4

Michael was on the operating table a little more than eight hours. We had two updates from the operating room, and I never left his hospital room as I waited to hear that everything went well.

But at about six o'clock, a nurse came to tell me Michael was going to the surgical intensive care unit because he was having trouble breathing. The ICU was two floors below the surgical unit, and it seemed like I was there in two steps, just in time to see him being wheeled in.

He was struggling to breathe, on oxygen, hooked up to monitors, and had surgical drains coming out from four incisions. He looked so frail and helpless.

I went to touch his face to let him know I was there, but I wasn't allowed to touch him. In fact, I was only allowed to be in the room with him for ten minutes every two hours. It was a barbaric policy that was supposed to allow the nurses and doctors to do their work more efficiently, but Michael was terrified every time he woke up. He couldn't have his blanket or his mother— the two things that comforted him the most. That couldn't have helped his healing. In fact, I'm sure his condition was made worse by his fear and stress.

So, while Michael was in ICU, Dave and Dr. Jack Amie, the chief resident in the urology department, spent most of their time with him so he wouldn't feel alone and frightened.

When I went upstairs to what had been Michael's room, our belongings had been cleared out by the nurses, so I spent my time in the waiting room. "He's not coming back up and we need the room," one nurse told me dismissively. "We need you to take everything out of here now."

In the morning, I would report the event, but that evening, Hazen and I had to clear all our belongings out of the hospital—clothes, toys, books, crocheting—all of it. There was no place to store any of it since Michael was in ICU.

Hazen tried to be comforting, but it didn't work. In desperation, he told me we could have another child if Michael died.

Another child. As though Michael could be replaced, I thought.

No one could replace those big, blue eyes with their constant mischievous gleam. That little baby chuckle was unique, as was his squeaky little voice, which spoke words most sixteen-month-old children couldn't pronounce yet. He was scary-smart, and I wanted to see where that brilliance would lead. No child could replace Michael. I was appalled that Hazen didn't know that. Was he ashamed of Michael's birth defect? He had mentioned more than once that nothing like this had ever happened in his family. He didn't know how to handle it.

"You just get up and go," I told him. "You have no choice but to handle it."

He said he no longer believed in God because a merciful God would never cause such pain to an innocent child.

I asked whether he ever had been aware of the pain and suffering in the world, or if he just looked at his own life as though he somehow deserved to get through life pain-free. I knew I wasn't being fair, but I didn't care.

Instead of going to bed, I went back to the hospital and slept in the ICU waiting room. I had a book and my crocheting with me, and the droning of the television was the white noise that helped drown out the pages and bells.

The next morning Michael's breathing wasn't any better and the doctors were beginning to worry about pneumonia, which—if he contracted—he wouldn't have the strength to fight. He wanted to be with me and cried a feeble, wheezing cry every time I had to leave the room, which didn't help his respiratory problems.

On the third day, the doctors told me he had the first signs on pneumonia, and they didn't want to give him steroids because of his size and if he had a bad reaction to them, he would die. They gave him a one in-four chance of surviving.

Hour after hour I heard pages and monitors; people came and went and I got up every two hours and went in to spend ten minutes with my son.

The lights were always on at the same level and there were no windows in the waiting room. Like so many people in ICU, I lost track of time. Hazen came and went, spending a couple hours every day with Danny and running errands. He's never been a man who could sit still for any length of time, and he knew I would be there for Michael.

I slept and awoke, listened to the noises of the ICU, grabbed a bite to eat from the cafeteria when I got hungry, and tried to read.

Dave promised he wouldn't let Michael die, and I believed him despite what the pulmonary doctor told me. But later in the day, things weren't improving. His breathing was still labored and he was starting to get fluid in his lungs.

After I saw him early in the evening, I went home to take a quick shower and change my clothes, praying all the way.

I remembered a story from church when I was little. It was about a mother who prayed for her sick son to live instead of praying for God's will to be done. The boy lived, but he grew up to be a criminal and the mother realized she should never have questioned God's plans.

I had long since given up the fundamentalist theology I was raised with, but this story came back to me, so I prayed, *God, I'm at my limit. I can't keep this up. Please do whatever it is you're going to do tonight. Either take him or give him back, but please do it tonight.*

#

The phone was ringing as I walked through the door. It was an ICU nurse. I didn't have time to take a breath before she told me not to worry.

"It's a miracle," she said. "I've never seen anything like it. One minute his breathing was terrible and the next minute he's fine. He's all pink and breathing fine. It's a miracle."

I raced back to the hospital to find him pulling off Dave's glasses and giggling. Dave leaned over the bed and Michael grabbed the glasses. Dave took them back, put them back on, and leaned over again; Mike grabbed and giggled. The game didn't get old.

"Look at him grab these glasses!" Dave said gleefully as I walked into the room (against the rules, but no one was going to keep me out). "He's fine."

Michael was back on the surgical floor the day after his breathing improved. He didn't want to eat. I tried to get him to eat by playing games with him. Still, he wouldn't eat and I was afraid he would lose weight again. When he knocked the bowl out of my hand, I held both his hands with one of mine and tried to get him to open his mouth so I could feed him with the other. As I turned to get a spoonful of food, I pulled him forward and he cried out.

I was nearly hysterical. I couldn't pick him up easily without causing him pain, so I held his hands and kissed his face over and over, promising him I would never hurt him again. Here I was the one who was supposed to be protecting him and I had hurt him. I had lost patience and gotten careless. What kind of a mother does that, anyway? How could I have lost sight of his needs and allowed my frustration to result in his being hurt?

When he fell asleep a few minutes later, I left the room and walked the floor for a half hour or more. I didn't want to go far because I knew he wouldn't sleep long and I needed to be there if he wanted anything.

He would spend another week in the hospital. I stayed with him, learning how to change his dressings—and otherwise be his nurse.

Dave and Matt both reassured me that I was the best nurse Michael could have. Their pep talks helped me hang on and take care of Michael. I was exhausted, but I was grateful that the worst of his reconstructive surgery was over. Once he got the brace off in six weeks, he would be facing a normal childhood.

Chapter 5

After Michael was home, I thought I would feel better, but Hazen said he didn't want me to leave Michael's side for at least another six months. He didn't trust anyone else to care for him. I sank into a deep depression.

Many mornings I didn't even open the drapes. I did what I had to do to care for the kids—but nothing more—because I couldn't force myself to care about anything but them. Hazen was blissfully unaware because of the hours he worked. As far as he knew, I was a bit of a lousy housekeeper, but everything else was fine.

Life settled into a dull, unchanging routine. Most days, weather permitting, we spent at least a little time outside, but it did nothing to lift my spirits.

#

I met Judy as I walked around the apartment complex with the kids one day. She was a psychologist and an Army wife. Because of a brain aneurism that occurred several months before we met, she wasn't able to work full time. She was eager to be practicing again, so she treated my depression without ever telling me she was doing so.

She came over in the morning and opened the drapes, turned off the television, and made me do something—anything. We folded laundry, took walks, cooked, talked, and played with the kids. She got me playing tennis, and my self-esteem started to rise.

By this time I had a car—a school-bus yellow Austin America that used almost as much oil as it did gas. We paid $1,000 for it, which was about twice what it was worth. But it was mine and I could take Michael to doctors' appointments without the grueling 5:00 a.m. to 7:00 p.m. runaround. Hazen's father called it a rolling death trap because it was so small, but I didn't care. I had a modicum of freedom as long as the car was running. My mechanic, Ashley Weeks, kept it running for over a year. Now whenever I see a Mini Cooper, I think of that little car.

#

Hazen's parents came to visit after Michael's surgery. They decided to take Hazen and Danny on a golf outing. Michael and I weren't invited because Michael wasn't strong enough to spend an entire day out of the house. Actually, he was, but Hazen was afraid of a medical emergency even when there was no chance of one.

So, Michael and I went for a ride, had a picnic lunch, and went to the mall, where I bought a $2 seashell necklace.

Laura had a fit. How dare I spend money on myself when we didn't know what Michael's medical bills would be?

Until now, I had avoided arguing with her. I knew she was stubborn and I usually just walked away. But this time I was furious. They had just spent a couple of hundred dollars on an outing that Michael and I had not been invited to attend. I almost never bought anything for myself and this necklace had cost only $2.

I defended my purchase and she continued to criticize me as a mother who didn't care about my child. Hazen stayed silent.

Things were getting out of hand until the Chief said something I never heard him say before or after.

"Laura, shut up."

She turned to him, stunned.

"I said shut up," he repeated. "That's enough."

She backed down and I put Michael in the stroller and took him out for a walk.

#

A few months after Michael's surgery, we moved to a bigger apartment closer to the paper mill where Hazen worked. This was in the days before scrubbers and other anti-pollution devices that reduced the sulfur spewed into the air. The neighborhood often smelled like rotten eggs, and the odor permeated everything. Even when I kept the windows closed, the smell was evident.

Even though the apartment and the entire neighborhood were nice, we were in the flight path of the Augusta airport. It's a little like living near a railroad track—after a while you don't notice the noise.

We settled in and got to know the neighbors. I found new tennis partners and Hazen worked.

I still wanted more in my life. I wanted to go back to school, do volunteer work, get a job. Hazen wanted a stay-at-home wife, and he controlled the purse strings. He went grocery shopping with me, sometimes bringing his calculator and often complaining that I was buying name brands when store brands were available. He wanted me to be more careful with his hard-earned money.

He was old-fashioned and I was becoming a feminist. After all we had been through with Michael, I realized that I was strong, I was intelligent, and I deserved a little more say in family decisions. I wanted to go to work, but he didn't want people thinking he couldn't support his family. I told him I would tell anyone who asked that he made plenty of money to support the family; he was not amused.

So we compromised. I took a real estate law class, a semester-long course that prepared students to take the real estate sales license exam. Classes were in the evening, so he could stay home with the boys or we could hire a sitter and he could go out.

I don't think he believed I could pass the exam—only about 15 percent of people taking it for the first time passed—but I did. When the results came in the mail, I was at the grocery store, so he opened the letter and announced it to me when I got home.

I was excited about passing the exam, but I was angry that he had opened a letter addressed to me.

"It wasn't to you," I said. "I need to have some boundaries. I'm an adult and when mail comes addressed to me, I need to be the one to open it."

He couldn't understand why I was upset, which only upset me more.

Was it unreasonable to expect that I should open my own mail? I didn't want to keep secrets, but I did want some privacy. I wanted to enjoy opening that letter myself after I had worked so hard to pass that test.

I had a job lined up: three mornings a week at Star Realty—and any other work I wanted to do, I could do from home. Danny was in nursery school and Michael stayed with a neighbor who had a son his age. The arrangement was perfect. I could work as few or as many hours as I wanted because I worked for commissions.

When I got my first business card, I marveled at my name on the card. It didn't say "Hazen's wife" or "Danny and Michael's mommy." There, in beautiful script, was "Leslie Danforth, real estate sales associate."

I had heard "OK, Hazen's wife sits here," or "This is Danny and Michael's mommy," too many times. Before I got that job, it seemed I would go days without hearing my own name.

#

Hazen's job had become difficult. His boss—I'll call him Willy—was an overbearing, sexist bully who liked to fire people on a whim. Hazen was good at his job, but that didn't matter to Willy. You bowed to his whims and hoped be didn't fire you because he didn't like the way you dressed that day.

Even though Hazen didn't like parties, we went to every company party or dinner because Willy might fire someone for being antisocial. I kept my distance from him, but one night, we came face-to-face.

"She's lovely," he said over my head. "What do you have her doing?"

"I sell real estate," I said. He continued to look over my head at Hazen.

"She sells real estate," Hazen said.

"Oh, I let my wife go to school," he said.

He asked a couple more questions about me and ignored my answers. Hazen was becoming uncomfortable at my insistence on answering, but I was getting steamed.

"Excuse me," I said finally. "I walk; I talk. I can hear and answer questions. Talk to me."

His expression darkened. "I have no respect for a man who can't control his wife."

"Well, I have no respect for a man who feels he has to," I answered.

Willy didn't like me, and that put Hazen's job in danger.

Not for long, though.

#

A few weeks after the party, I was walking around the apartment complex with the boys, and as I rounded the corner of the building with the apartment rented by the company for visiting executives and job applicants, a little sports car drove up and a lovely young woman stepped out and let herself into the apartment.

Not five minutes later, a second car drove up and Willy got out, a bottle of wine under his arm.

I called to him and waved and he blanched.

"Oh, I, uh, forgot my keys," he said, turning toward his car.

"That shouldn't be a problem," I said. "I'm sure that nice lady who got here a couple minutes ago would let you in."

He fumbled with the car door and got back in.

"Oh, if you see Hazen, would you ask him to pick up some milk?" I hollered as he drove away.

Hazen came home that evening and I asked where the milk was.

"I asked Willy to tell you to pick some up."

The color drained from his face.

"What. Have. You. Done?"

"Nothing," I said. "I saw Willy about to go into the company apartment with a bottle of wine under his arm a couple minutes after a really lovely young woman arrived. I just said hello and then he got in his car, and I figured he'd probably see you this afternoon and all, so I asked him to give you the message."

Hazen's job was safe. In fact, Willy was downright friendly after that. I would never have told his wife, but he didn't know that.

It's one of my favorite moments. I don't like bullies.

Hazen still wanted to get out of that paper mill, though, and when a former boss and friend called to offer him a job in suburban West Nyack, New York, he was ready to bolt before he hung up the phone.

I wasn't ready to be pulled up by the roots, however. Our marriage was in trouble and I wanted to concentrate on counseling before we made any big changes in our lives. But Hazen didn't believe in counseling. He didn't want to tell his problems to some nosy person who wanted his money as well as his dirty laundry.

The kids and I had friends in Augusta. I had a part-time job that I could go to full time if I had to. I didn't want to leave.

But he took the job and started talking about it as "our decision."

How could it be our decision if I was so against it?

"I listened to your input and made the final decision, so it's our decision," he said.

I was through, but he didn't believe it.

Chapter 6

Hazen moved to New York, leaving me—he thought—to tie up loose ends in Augusta. I intended to stay.

The decision was made for me a couple of weeks later, though.

I was at a red light behind a tanker truck when a fully loaded dump truck rear-ended me after its brakes failed.

The boys always called it the ice cream accident because it happened next to an ice cream stand. After people who saw the accident pulled me and my terrified toddlers out of the car, someone decided they could be calmed down with a dish of homemade, hand-dipped ice cream.

It worked. As soon as the kids saw I was OK and the ice cream was in front of them, they were fine.

But I sustained a neck injury that kept me from working or even being able to care for the kids properly. Because I worked on commission and had been working less than a year, I had no way to prove to a court that I had lost income. In Georgia at the time, that's how damages were decided. It didn't even matter that the trucking company had been cited previously for having bad brakes on its trucks.

So, we moved to New York in July 1977.

As we left Augusta, Danny chirped, "Are we halfway there yet?" At age four and a half, he had discovered the concept of half. He wanted to eat half his dinner, then half of that, then half of that . . .

"No," I answered. "It's a very long drive and we won't even be halfway there for a long time."

"Oh. Then are we halfway to halfway there?"

"Not yet."

It was the halfway to halfway to halfway to halfway . . . challenge and I would be hounded until I estimated the halfway to eternity point. I didn't want to lie and raise his expectations, so I told him we were staying in a motel and when we got there, we would be halfway to New York.

"Are we halfway to the motel then?"

"Not yet."

We settled for halfway to halfway to halfway to halfway to the motel, which we probably were by the time the conversation ended to his satisfaction.

#

I missed my friends in Georgia, but being in New York made it easier to get home to see my folks in Massachusetts. Michael took to my father immediately. His grandpa was Michael's hero, and my father loved being adored. For all the trouble Hazen had dealing with Michael's physical problems, my father could overlook them and see Michael as a bright, overactive, funny kid.

Danny never enjoyed the trips to New England as much as Michael did because he hated being in the car for three hours or more, and he was never as impulsive as my family. He wanted to know what to expect and when; he hated surprises and he hated spur-of-the-moment anything.

He and my mother were closer because she was more like him. She understood the value of having a plan. The rest of us just wanted to explore the possibilities before committing to a plan—or better yet, plunge in and see what happened.

My stepmother was the perfect buddy for Michael. She spent most weekends dressed up as a clown entertaining children and adults and she was the most impulsive member of the family. Barbara believes in finding adventure every day, and she usually stumbles across something interesting and fun in her travels. She and my father often got into the car and drove until one of them had an idea where they might go.

Michael and my older sister Ellen's daughter, Shannon, were best friends before the first weekend visit was over.

Ellen and I took the kids for a walk in the woods behind her house. As we were walking back, Shannon stopped at a fork in the path.

"Which way do we go?" she asked.

Michael pointed to the right and Ellen praised him for remembering so well.

Shannon gazed adoringly at him and sighed, "Oh, Michael, you're so smart. You know *everything!*"

Mike always said that was the moment Shannon became his favorite cousin, and the joke lasted the rest of his life. If they disagreed, he brought up the walk in the woods and Shannon would at least pretend to agree.

After Ellen and her husband divorced, we still went to the house on weekends so Michael could see Shannon.

Being in New York meant we could finally make it to the family Christmas party every year. The Sunday before Christmas, all five of Daddy's kids, all seven of Barbara's kids (the Phipps clan), spouses and children, gathered at Daddy's house. We numbered between twenty-five and forty, depending on whether friends came along.

The party was too much for Hazen, who didn't like the commotion and never felt comfortable among the Boyd-Phipps crowd. That first year, he stayed for an hour, went for a long walk, and then announced it was time for us to leave because he had to work the next day. It would be his only Boyd-Phipps party.

That Christmas, I bought myself a Christmas present—a Guild guitar. Since Hazen kept a tight rein on the finances, all of my income went straight into his checking account and he made all the decisions about where it would be spent. While I hate anything to do with finances, I did want some say in how our money was spent. So I got myself the guitar to replace my old cheap one. It was expensive, but Hazen had just bought a console color TV for himself, so he didn't complain too much. He rarely bought gifts for me because he believed Christmas and birthdays were for children. Now, when I sang the boys to sleep, the accompaniment would sound wonderful.

\#

Hazen and I split in January 1978. He had insisted we didn't need counseling and that the move to New York was all we needed to make a fresh start. But the move didn't make things better. In fact, I resented the hell out of it.

But now I was in New York. I promised myself the move would be temporary, that I wouldn't live in the suburbs of New York City for long. Well, long is relative; I lived there for twenty-five years, and Michael was the quintessential New York kid, right down to his accent, his rather foul mouth, and his inexplicable love of the New York Yankees.

I met and started dating Tim Joyce, a New Jersey native who loved the New York Yankees (maybe that's where my kids got it). The boys loved him, even though he was "not-dad."

Tim was very ticklish, and he and the boys played a game to see who could keep a straight face the longest while being tickled. Tim lasted about thirty seconds and Danny about ten. Michael was on the floor squealing, "Stop!" before anyone even touched him.

When Tim was around, the kids were almost always with us because I couldn't afford babysitters, and he seemed to enjoy the boys as much as they liked him. He was a good playmate for all of us, and we remained friends after we broke up two and a half years later.

Tim got along well with the rest of my family, too, mainly because he never got mad at Ellen's practical jokes or Daddy's curmudgeonly ways. In fact, the two of them worked on crossword puzzles—in ink—in silence on Sunday mornings. We had to buy two copies of the paper. Often, Michael sat nearby, trying to be quiet. He wanted to be one of the curmudgeons.

My father always pretended to hate Christmas and would "Bah! Humbug!" on command for the children, who weren't fooled by his act. He dressed up in his red corduroy shirt and held court at the head of the table—Santa without the beard or the hair and with a really bad attitude.

Many of my favorite childhood memories are of extended family gatherings, and my boys hadn't had any experience with that until the 1977 party. The adults gathered in the kitchen and the children went off to play in the family room, sneaking upstairs occasionally to listen to what the adults were talking about.

I remember hearing my parents and aunts and uncles laughing at jokes I didn't understand, and my kids remember us poking fun at each other as we smoked cigarettes and drank cup after cup after cup of coffee.

I finally became closer to my sisters. Ellen and I had been rivals since my birth. I have a picture of her kneeling beside her bed, praying—my grandmother told me she was praying for a little sister. Once I arrived, though, she discovered she wasn't the center of the universe anymore. Everyone wanted to see the baby. People brought gifts for the baby, and she was sent off to play while the adults—and the baby—visited. It didn't take long for her to resent me.

Once I was living closer and visiting often, our fierce rivalry became mostly a joke. We became co-conspirators on practical jokes aimed at family and friends.

We convinced one of her friends that I was a PhD candidate in human sexual behavior and I was conducting a study of certain marital behaviors for my dissertation.

Ellen went in first; I waited a few minutes before I rang the doorbell and put on my best southern accent. I introduced myself as Precious Calhoun, and in my southern accent I asked if they would take my survey. They both agreed, and as the questions became more outrageous, so did Ellen's answers. Her friend became increasingly uncomfortable until she finally just fell apart.

Ellen and I spent a lot of time on those questions. I loved being her partner in crime.

I loved being able to let my kids get to know my family and see the places I used to go as a kid. I took them to Cape Cod in the winter, showed them where I went to school, and where we bought penny candy. I brought them to the apple farm in Sheldonville, where I spent my formative years. It wasn't an apple farm anymore, but we could still walk into the woods near where the Nolans had lived.

Mr. Nolan was a lion tamer and in the summer, his lions were kept in a large cage on his property. We fell asleep at night to the sounds of their roars. My father told us that the lions' teeth had been pulled and they were harmless, so we came to love that sound. After we moved to North Attleboro—a town where you could hear your neighbors if they raised their voices—people didn't believe we had lived down the road from lions.

The Nolan house burned down sometime in the seventies and the family sold the property to the town for a park. So we could walk into Joe's Rock, a cliff that overlooked much of Sheldonville, from a parking lot near the road and without crossing private property. We could see the old cranberry bog and the Wheelers' dairy farm, pastures and orchards, and the pasture pine where we took our library books on summer afternoons and relaxed in the shade.

I wanted my kids to be able to touch my childhood so they could understand how I became who I am. I wanted the stories I told them to come alive because they had seen the places where things happened.

Even as adults they talked about "the pink store" by the school. That was the Falls Market, which was painted bright pink. It was within walking distance of my father's house, so we made a few trips there to get treats. It was torn down in the late eighties; a bank stands on the corner now.

As we walked the half mile back to my father's house, I could name the family that had occupied each house along the route . . . the Glodes, the Larsons, the Trepanias, the McKitchens, the Morses . . . and tell stories about each one. I was also able to do that for just about every house between the apple farm and the general store in Sheldonville.

The building that had housed the farm store and cider mill had become a house, so I imagine a pool table was standing where I used to load apples into the crusher for 25 cents a day. I had to explain to the kids that a quarter was a lot of money to me in 1959—it could buy five candy bars, or three candy bars and a soda. I could also earn money by riding the old hay rake, which was harder than it sounds. I sat on the seat and then, every few seconds, pushed down the foot pedal to raise the tines, leaving a pile of hay on the ground. The baler would come along later to bind it up.

Sitting on the hay rake was brutal on hot summer afternoons. Whoever was on the rake usually wore a straw hat to keep the sun off, but legs and arms usually got pretty well burned.

By the time Danny was in third grade, he was learning "sun safety," or how to prevent melanoma later on in life, and he asked why we didn't use sunscreen when I was young.

"We didn't have it," I said. To both boys, that sounded like I was raised in the Dark Ages.

Yes, I keep a watch on my skin for evidence of cancers, but I still think worse damage was done to my body by riding the DDT wagon. We rode the wagon through the orchard as the farmhands sprayed the trees. We came home white with the powder dried on our clothes and skin.

Even though most of the apple trees were gone, the new owners gave me permission to take the boys around the farm. At the top of the orchard, which had become a horse pasture (later it would become a housing development), was a steep hill. That was where we went sledding. Sometimes, someone would bring a toboggan, and once, Ellen persuaded me to ride it with her.

"The safest place is in the front," she said.

So I climbed aboard with her behind me and we took off.

To steer a toboggan, you lean toward the direction you wish to turn. What we didn't know was that it is nearly impossible to steer on sharp turns, so we slammed into one of the apple trees that we'd always been able to avoid on our sleds. I got two black eyes, and Ellen got in trouble for making me ride in front when she knew it wasn't the safest place.

"No wonder she hated you," Danny said. "You were always getting her in trouble."

"Well, she was always trying to kill me," I said.

Late one afternoon, I got stuck in the upper branches of a golden delicious tree in the orchard, out of hollering range of the house. Ellen left, saying she was going to get help. Instead, she went home, and when suppertime came and my parents asked where I was, Ellen said she didn't know.

If one of the farmhands, an older man named Ira, hadn't heard my cries and come to my rescue with a ladder, I'd have been there until . . . well, I don't know how long I would've been there.

Ellen hadn't thought far enough ahead to plan a defense, so—again—she was the one who got in trouble. Had I figured out how to get down and come home, Ellen probably would have said she had no idea that I was stuck and I would have had to go to bed without supper.

Of course, I had to pass the hard-ass attitude along to a younger sibling. One winter evening, Robin and I were home alone. It was snowing, and I bet her I could beat her in a race to the stone wall at the back of our yard. We would go outside in what we were wearing (pajamas and slippers) and race, and I would give her a head start.

She took the bait. We stood on the back steps, I shouted, "Go!" and she took off. I turned around and went back into the house, locking the door behind me. I figured she'd yell; I would make her wait a few seconds and then I'd let her in. I hadn't counted on her breaking a windowpane in the door and reaching in to unlock it. If my parents hadn't come home just then, I'm sure she would have kicked the crap out of me. She's three years younger, but she's strong.

A couple of years later, Danny played the same trick on Michael, who never thought to break a windowpane in the door. Instead, he had to stand outside for three minutes—in his underwear—before Danny let him back in.

That's what I got for telling funny stories about my childhood to my kids.

#

It was about this time that I met Danielle, who owned a small bar and restaurant with her brothers and sister. We hit it off immediately because we were both badass women. We were both divorced and she had a daughter, Colette, a little younger than Michael. The two of them got along well, and Michael and Danny thought of Danielle as another aunt.

The bar, Dubonnay's, had an open-mike comedy night, and I decided to try my hand at stand-up comedy. For the next several months, Danielle and I traveled to nightclubs around the area until I got tired of hearing bad jokes, the late nights, and creepy club managers' come-ons.

She came with me to visit my family in Massachusetts and she fit right in. We were pretty much inseparable when we weren't working. When Michael was in the hospital, she picked up Danny after school and took him to her house for supper.

I was waiting for her at the bar one night when a vendor struck up a conversation with me. I explained I was waiting for a friend. He said he was waiting to talk to the owner, who was a bitch.

"That's the friend I'm waiting for," I said. "What makes her a bitch?"

Well, she wanted her own way on everything and she reported him to his boss for being rude to her. He was there to apologize.

"Doesn't sound like you're terribly sorry to me," I said. "Maybe your problem is that you don't like having a woman making you do things her way." That probably put me in his bitch category as well, and for a while, Danielle and I called ourselves *The Bitches*.

Danielle is an artist and she's very adept at picking up junk furniture and making it beautiful. She taught me to shop at thrift stores in wealthy neighborhoods since that's where the pickings were best. I found a nearly new suede coat for $20, just in time for a job interview.

As always, Michael was good at leaving a mess wherever he went. One night, he and Colette tore her room apart. They took out every toy, every book, and all the arts and crafts supplies. When it was almost time for us to leave, I went upstairs to survey the damage. Danielle and I demanded that they pick up the mess immediately, and Colette put her little hands on her hips.

"What do I look like, the maid?" she demanded. Immediately, she knew she had gone too far.

"Michael, you and your mom can go now," Danielle said. "The maid is going to clean the room herself."

Danielle is a strong presence in our lives, even today. She lives in Texas and I'm in North Carolina, but we talk frequently. She would become one of Michael's strongest allies. For a time, she and I were the only two people who believed he would straighten out.

Chapter 7

A couple of years after we moved to New York, Hazen took a job in Brunswick, Georgia, halfway between Savannah, Georgia, and Jacksonville, Florida. Before he left, he told Danny he would have loved for all of us to go together, but Mommy wouldn't come. Looking back, I don't think he meant to be vindictive. I think he really was just trying to explain to the kid why we all weren't going together, but the result was a very angry, resentful seven-year-old.

When the boys' father moved, we agreed he would take them for a few weeks during the summer, and if he wanted them on alternate holidays, all he had to do was come pick them up or pay for airfare since he was the one who moved and he was the one making a decent income.

The first summer, the boys were five and seven, and he came to pick them up. After they drove away, with the boys smiling and waving through the back window of Hazen's Honda Civic, I went into the house to find Michael's blanket on the couch.

I crocheted that bright green and yellow blanket before Michael was born and it had been with him every time he went to sleep. It was with him in the hospital even when I wasn't; it came along on vacations. I knew he wouldn't sleep without it.

At about nine o'clock that night, Hazen called. I could hear Michael wailing in the background.

"I'll mail the blanket," I said.

"No," he insisted. "FedEx the damn thing! I'll pay!"

Coming from Hazen, that was something; he was a notorious tightwad. The boys used to joke that when their dad opened his wallet, moths flew out.

The blanket fell apart when Michael was ten. I remember him coming upstairs from the family room, wailing as though someone had just died. Danny wanted to throw the pieces away, but I let Michael hang onto them until I could crochet a twin-size blanket, this one in royal blue and bright red. We jokingly called it his "boo bankie."

That first summer, Hazen returned the boys home with home-cut hair. Danny's was OK, but Michael looked like he had done the job himself. Only a professional should attempt to cut the hair of a kid who can't sit still.

The night they left, I had a vivid dream that still haunts me. I was in a cemetery looking at Michael's gravestone and I couldn't stop crying. I felt an overwhelming despair.

I suspected from that night on that I would outlive him.

Day care wasn't easy for Michael—partly because all of the children were forced to nap after lunch. Michael wasn't a napper. He was forced to be still and quiet for an hour—something totally against his nature. If he fell asleep, it meant he wasn't going to bed before 11:00 p.m. that night, or else he would wake up at 3:00 a.m.

I had to sleep with one eye open because nothing could be put out of his reach—he was a climber. As a toddler, one of his favorite tricks was to pour shampoo into the toilet and flush it to see the bubbles.

I didn't want him well rested at bedtime, yet an afternoon nap caused just that.

I asked whether he could be allowed to read or color and was told that all the children must nap after lunch. There wasn't any wiggle room in the rules.

The child care center closed at 5:30 p.m.; it charged a dollar a minute for anyone who was late, and the director didn't want to release my children to anyone but me. But I didn't get off work until 5:30 p.m.

Again, there was no wiggle room in the rules. I fought the director and she agreed to let me hire one of the day care center workers to take the boys home with her until I could get there at 6:00 p.m.

We battled on and off for a year before I finally found a woman who would look after the boys for the same price as the center, an elderly African American woman named Beatrice Muckle. She and her husband had been foster parents to more than thirty children. They didn't think they were young enough to take in any more foster children, but they were eager to look after my boys.

If one of the kids was sick, Mrs. Muckle would make weak tea and chicken soup. It was she who introduced us to collards, grits done right, and real iced tea. My boys and I adored her.

Michael's health was better than the doctors had predicted. His "plumbing" left him very vulnerable to kidney infections, but he hadn't had even one, and his kidneys continued to develop normally. Overall, he was enjoying a pretty normal childhood.

Michael's school career started with a kindergarten teacher who thought he was wonderful in spite of his hyperactivity and impulsivity.

"He's all boy," she told me at our first meeting. "More all boy than most boys."

He was also "scary-smart." He could absorb knowledge on the run and it didn't seem to bother her that his learning style could be disruptive to others in the class. Apparently, it didn't matter much in kindergarten—although it would in first grade.

By this time, we were living in Chestnut Ridge, New York. Mrs. Muckle was too far away to look after the boys anymore. There were no after-school programs. I was working for a weekly newspaper making very little money. I was paying $350 a month for rent, $35 for telephone, $100 for a car payment, $75 for electricity—at the end of the week I had about $25 for groceries. There was no way I could pay for after-school care for both kids.

That's when Danny became a latchkey kid. He was seven. Our upstairs neighbor kept an eye on him when she was home. Fortunately, she was home most afternoons. I worked five minutes away and could get home if there was an emergency. Again, fortunately, there never was one.

I applied to the Department of Social Services to try and get a child care subsidy, but I was turned down because I wasn't receiving Aid to Dependent Children. To receive that, I would have had to leave my job and get trapped into a governmental system that I had no interest in being in. It was better to struggle and to try to make my own way—although I know Danny didn't think so at the time.

It didn't make sense to me and eventually it changed, but for the time being, Danny would have to be at home alone for two hours every afternoon while Michael had a babysitter.

Michael had one more major surgery to go—an operation to close the split in his penis. The surgery was pretty straightforward, but he had to be virtually immobile for ten days so it would heal properly. I brought piles of books, puzzles, and games to the hospital.

On the days Danny came with me to see him, he pushed Michael around the floor on a gurney so he could visit other patients, and the two of them played and watched TV together. On other days, Danny went to Danielle's house, where he ate a good dinner and played with Colette.

When it finally came time to take off the bandages, Michael looked down at his repaired penis, looked up at his doctor and said, "I thought you were going to make it bigger."

"It starts early," his doctor told me.

#

The boys were six and eight when I met Rob in May of 1980. It was not love at first sight. He thought I was an overbearing, brassy broad and I thought he was a cranky intellectual snob.

In October, my stepbrother, Marc Phipps, was killed in an auto accident. It was devastating for everyone in the family. Marc was a kind and gentle man, more quiet than his brothers, but always willing to take part in the mischief.

On November 3, everyone forgot Mike's and my birthday. In my family, your birthday is your own personal national holiday. It's a huge deal, and I hadn't gotten a single card. I understood why everyone had forgotten, but it was just another reason to be sad.

Rob and I were working for the same weekly newspaper, and when he realized it was my birthday, he went out at lunchtime and bought me a card and a little gift.

Nine days later, we started dating. On our second date, Rob mentioned he played softball in the summer and nothing was going to get in the way of that, and that his friends were important to him. They had been friends since fourth grade; they grew up together; they played softball together and they vacationed together every summer on Long Beach Island at the Jersey Shore. As they all began to date and marry, the women became part of the group, and the whole group would become extended family to me and my boys.

Michael loved having Rob come over because while I was cooking dinner, Rob would read to Michael. Danny, on the other hand, wasn't so pleased. He had loved Tim, but Tim and I had been broken up for almost a year. I think he still had fantasies of his father and I getting back together, and Rob would just be standing in the way. When Rob and I married, on November 12, 1983, Danny's dream of a reconciliation was finally put to rest.

"Oh, is *he* here again?" Danny asked one day when he came into the house. "When is he leaving?"

Rob went out to his car and got his softball glove and asked if Danny wanted to toss the ball around while I made supper. Danny warmed up to him a little, but their relationship would always be a rocky one until Danny was married with a daughter.

By the time he was in second grade, Michael had a reputation as a wild kid. He couldn't sit still, although he continued to do well scholastically. He tested in the top first or second percentile in both language and mathematical abilities, but his inability to sit still and his impulsivity were distractions to his classmates.

His teacher told me, "He's slow."

"Really? His problem is that he can't slow down," I said.

"No, I mean intellectually," she said.

I reminded her of his test scores and the fact that in second grade he was reading at a fifth grade level.

I requested he be tested for attention deficit hyperactivity disorder (ADHD), but the school turned me down, despite the fact federal law required he be tested. I was a single mother; I couldn't afford an attorney, and they knew it.

I asked for a hearing and finally got one, although I had to take a day off without pay to attend. I was seated at a low table facing the principal, superintendent, school psychologist, and a couple of other people who were seated at a dais above me. I was the only person at floor level.

The principal started off by saying he was reluctant to label children, but I argued that if a child has a condition it needs to be diagnosed so he isn't *mis*labeled as bad.

The psychologist suggested Michael would be better behaved if I spent more time with him.

I was so angry by this point that I was shaking. I did something that surprised even me.

I stood up, and when the school psychologist asked where I was going, I told him I thought I'd poke around the building and see if I could find someone competent to talk to.

His face reddened. "How dare you suggest I'm incompetent," he choked.

I glared at him. "Look, you just suggested I'm a bad mother. I took a day off without pay to come here and beg for help for my son and all I hear is that I'm to blame. You are in violation of federal law and because I can't afford a lawyer, you think you can bully me."

I told them I was through cooperating with them. At home he would be my problem, but as long as they wouldn't live up to their end of the deal and obey federal law, I didn't want to hear another word from them. I told them I would not respond to calls saying he had created a distraction in class.

I stood up and left.

A few days later, the principal called.

"Oh, have you decided to have my son evaluated?" I asked.

"Now, we've been all through that," he said.

I hung up.

A while later, the superintendent called to say he was considering expelling Michael.

As luck would have it, I had a friend who had just passed the New York State Bar exam. She offered to make a call. We both knew it wouldn't take any more than that to make them see the light.

When she reached the superintendent, he said he knew I couldn't afford an attorney.

"I know," my friend said. "That's why I'm taking the case pro bono. Do you have any idea how much trouble we're going to cause you?"

Suddenly, his attitude changed. Of course Michael would be evaluated.

"Don't bother," my friend said. "They're moving out of the district."

We moved across the state line into Bergen County, New Jersey, where Michael was evaluated within three weeks and placed in a small class with language lab desks to minimize distractions. But the school was on the other end of the county and Michael had to take the short bus. If I drove him to school, he had to get up earlier and he would get to school thirty minutes early, but he was happy with that.

Before long, though, I was under pressure to put him on drugs. Back then, it was believed that Ritalin, the drug of choice, stopped working once ADHD kids reached adulthood, so I didn't want to comply. I was told I would be reported to Child Protective Services and could lose custody of my child if I continued to refuse.

By now my income level was a little better, mostly because Rob and I had moved in together. We could fight, but we decided to try the Ritalin for a few months.

Within six weeks, Michael complained he didn't like being on Ritalin.

"It makes me feel like I'm not me," he said.

After another few weeks, he began refusing to take it in the morning, so we made a deal.

"This is going to be really hard," I said, "but you have to prove you can be in control of your behavior. So, you work really hard and if you can do this, then we've proven you don't need the Ritalin."

It would be three months before his teacher called to say, "Somebody forgot to take his medicine this morning."

I admitted he hadn't taken the medicine in three months and that he would not be taking it again. The teacher, surprised at his stubborn aversion to the drug and to how long he had been able to control his impulsivity, agreed.

Still, he had to be steered to stay on task. I could tell Danny to clean his room and it would get done. Not so with Michael. I had to pop my head in the door every few minutes to see how he was doing. Invariably, he had gotten distracted.

Rob didn't fully understand why Michael seemed to get a pass on having to clean his room by himself. When Rob's mother told him to clean his room, he did it without any further prompting. But he came to realize that Michael wasn't being disobedient; he just couldn't stay on task without the reminders.

Any complex task had to be broken down into smaller bits. We couldn't just tell him to clean his room; we had to start with, "Get everything out from under your bed." From there, we moved on to putting his dirty clothes in the hamper, gathering the books and putting them in the bookcase, and finally to putting all the toys into the toy box.

Homework was a huge challenge. If he had put as much energy into doing it as he put into avoiding it, we would have been fine. But he was stubborn. At one point, we had a notebook that went back and forth between the teachers and me. He was watched as he did the work, and as soon as things improved and we trusted him, he went back to not doing the work.

As Michael was entering middle school, we moved from Fair Lawn, New Jersey, to Stony Point, New York. Danny was miserable. He had put down roots in Fair Lawn and didn't want to move. But I had gotten a job at the *Journal-News* in West Nyack and Rob had been hired by the same company—but for a job in White Plains, across the Tappan Zee Bridge. The commute was an hour for him and forty minutes for me, so we rented a four-bedroom house with a huge yard exactly 2.1 miles from the high school. That meant Danny would have to walk.

North Rockland High School is a huge, sprawling complex more than a quarter mile long that had 2,300 students in 1987. It was intimidating, and it had the longest school day in New York State. Students had to be in homeroom at 7:10 a.m.

On top of that, the *Journal-News* was an afternoon paper, so if there was breaking news or a late meeting, I might work until 3:00 a.m. Having to get up again at 6:30 a.m. was a nightmare for me because I couldn't get back to sleep once I was up.

Fortunately, we had a neighbor who passed by at about 6:50 a.m., and if Danny was outside, he would give him a lift.

Michael saw the move as a new start. He had every intention of being in mainstream classes again and of being accepted.

We lived in Stony Point, but Michael was placed in classes in Haverstraw Middle School and assigned a psychologist, Russell Karkheck, who would save my sanity over the next six or so years. For the only time in his entire school career (at least until he made the Dean's List at Armstrong Atlantic State University), he made the honor roll.

He joined a Boy Scout troop in Stony Point, down the street from where we lived. He met Kevin, and that's when things started to fall apart.

People insisted when Michael was placed at Haverstraw Middle School that he would find trouble there. Haverstraw has been an immigrant village for more than one hundred years. It saw waves of Italians, Irish, Eastern Europeans, and finally Latinos.

In fact, Rob's uncle was among the Eastern European immigrants who worked in the brickyards there. The Catholic Church in Haverstraw had a Spanish Mass on Sunday. The vibrant downtown was filled with bodegas and small restaurants. In the summer, people escaped their hot apartments and sat outside, greeting each other and listening to music.

Although there were a lot of low-income families in the village, they were strong families. The children I came to know were almost always well behaved and well mannered.

Haverstraw was a great place for Michael. He got along well with the kids in his classes and loved the diversity. He even learned a few words of Spanish—most of them curse words as I recall. He learned to appreciate the different customs, and especially the foods. But the dire predictions of drug use and violence never touched him in Haverstraw.

In eighth grade, Mike was moved to Stony Point Middle School, and within a year, he and Kevin were using cigarettes, pot, and beer. Since my generation used pot, I wasn't really concerned when I discovered he was using it in high school.

I had a lot to learn.

I didn't know then that pot was twelve times more powerful than it was when I was young. I also didn't know that the younger kids are when they start using alcohol, the more likely they will become addicted. Michael told me later that he believes he was born an addict.

"The first drink I ever took affected me that way," he told me later. "I knew I wouldn't be able to stop."

Michael was adept at hiding his vices—he and Kevin hid their drug and alcohol use from Kevin's parents and from me—and I was adept at denial (much later we would call me Cleopatra, Queen of Denial). His behavior at school deteriorated, partly because the students in Stony Point were white and middle-class, and they weren't as accepting of his quirky sense of humor and impulsivity. I told him what my grandmother told me: that he saw the world from a different perspective than the rest of the kids, and while that might be difficult now, it would get better.

Although Michael met Kevin in Stony Point and became addicted to drugs and alcohol there, it was the Boy Scouts that kept him in touch with the way things ought to be. He had good troop leaders who appreciated his intelligence and, at least most of the time, his sense of humor. They took him on overnight hikes and camping trips that would keep him away from trouble for a little while.

In his freshman year of high school, Michael tried a couple of extracurricular activities. He played bass drum in the marching band and ran track for one year. But by his sophomore year, Boy Scouts was all that was left.

Each year, Michael's troop would have an event for the Cub Scouts who were about to move up a level. One year, Michael brought the telescope he had gotten for Christmas. He loved astronomy, and he wanted to share it with the Cub Scouts. Unfortunately, one of them broke it.

"Oh, fuck!" Michael said.

The child's mother rushed over.

"How dare you use such language at a church function! My little boy won't join this troop!"

First of all, I told her, this was a Boy Scout function, not a church function, and second, I thought my son deserved at least an apology for his broken telescope, which I couldn't afford to replace right then.

She poked her nose in the air and went off to complain to the scout leader, who agreed that Michael should apologize, but insisted that her son also apologize to Michael for breaking the telescope. We never saw her or her son again, although I did chastise Michael for dropping the f-bomb at a Boy Scout function.

"He fuckin' broke my telescope," Michael said.

Michael advanced through the ranks and made it to Life Scout, one rank shy of Eagle, before he got tired of it. The truth was, his addictions had begun to take over his entire life.

Russ Karkheck did his best to keep Michael in touch with reality; he also helped us to keep in touch with Michael.

"Talk *at* him if you have to," Russ said. "I know most psychologists won't tell you that, but I will. Just keep telling him what's right and let him know you're there if he needs anything."

So, I talked at him. He was going to church with Kevin's family and the pastor there was kind and nonjudgmental. Michael needed every helping hand there was during these years, and there were many people who reached out to him. After church, he and Kevin would go to a nearby street corner and buy pot for the week. Eventually, he would graduate to selling pot and using just about anything he could get his hands on. He referred to himself as a garbage head.

I had long ago given up the homework notebook. Michael had to learn to do what was required of him or fail. I had one teacher argue that I should be sitting down and doing his homework with him, but I believed then, and I still believe, that homework is a lesson in responsibility. I did my homework when I was in school; now it was Michael's turn to do his. If he had a question or a problem, I was happy to help, but I would not sit down and do his homework with him. When it came to homework, it was time for him to do it without being badgered.

Most teachers let him slide on the homework because he aced every test he took. They gave him Cs because he knew the material without doing the homework.

But in his sophomore year in high school, his English teacher called me a few weeks before the end of the school year. She had told the class at the beginning of the year that they would be expected to do a report, and that they could not get a passing grade without it. Michael had shown no evidence that he had even started the project and she wanted me to help him get it done.

I refused. I told her I did my homework and now it was his turn, that his failure to do the assignment wasn't because he needed help but because he was being lazy, and that if he didn't turn in the report, she needed to fail him.

"I really don't want to do that," she said.

"Well, he won't learn anything if you pass him without his completing the report, and he won't learn anything if I do the work for him," I said. "If he fails now, maybe he won't neglect to do assignments in the future, when a job could depend on it."

Michael failed the course by a quarter point, just as the teacher had said he would in the beginning of the year and several times during the year.

"What a bitch!" he said. "A quarter point and she couldn't give it to me."

"You didn't earn it," I said. "You knew the consequences and now you have to live with them."

As we struggled with Michael's reluctance to do homework, we also were having issues with Danny, who was still angry about having to move to Stony Point. We tried to get him to go to counseling, but he refused. The one time we got him to a counselor's office, he refused to speak to her.

His anger issues were disrupting the entire family. His father and I talked it over and I finally told Danny he had to agree to counseling or he could move in with his dad; staying with us and not getting counseling wasn't an option. It was a damn hard decision, but as long as the behavior patterns stayed the same, no one was going to be happy, least of all Danny.

So, when they left to visit their father in July 1988, only Michael had a round-trip ticket.

Danny and I actually talked more often after he left, and he was happier. When he did come back to visit, we got along well. He would still struggle for years, but it was only a few months after he arrived in Georgia before he met Jennifer, whom he would marry in 1992.

That spring, we moved into another house in Stony Point. It had four bedrooms, so I gave Michael first dibs. One of the rooms had a hideous bright red plaid carpet, and Michael chose it immediately.

"I can wear plaid and lie down on the carpet and all you'll see is my smile," he said. "It's my favorite color, you know."

Michael did wear a lot of plaid. It was the era of grunge and the kids were wearing plaid flannel shirts over black rock 'n' roll T-shirts and tattered blue jeans. He wanted to grow his hair and I told him if he kept it clean he could grow it.

In 1989, Rob and I were finally ready to buy a house. In New York, closing costs equaled about 10 percent of the price of the house, so to put 20 percent down, we needed to save 30 percent of the cost of a house. Rob's mother helped us get it all together.

"I don't want you waiting around for me to die so you can buy a house," she said. "I prefer to see you living in it and happy while I'm still here."

We started looking and almost immediately found an old center-hall colonial in Haverstraw.

"It's in the village, you know," the real estate agent said, figuring I would get the hint. The village is about 60 percent Latino.

"Yeah, I know," I said, "and it's illegal for you to try and steer us away."

One look at the place and we were sold. It was 106 years old and solid. The yard was a double lot and it had a magnificent old apple tree—a Winesap, my favorite. Under the ratty brown sculpted carpet was hardwood flooring. The woodwork had never been painted.

On the downside, the kitchen was old—1970s avocado appliances. The master bedroom was Pepto-Bismol pink and the half bath was finished with pink fixtures and dark paneling. But we knew we could update those things we didn't like.

The neighborhood was a mix of new and old inhabitants. A couple of families lived in the same house for two or three generations. My house was sold to me by the family that built it—the woman was the great-granddaughter of the original owner.

Diagonally across the street was a halfway house for people in recovery from addiction. The real estate agent hadn't told us about that, but I was happy to have them as neighbors. When it snowed, they came out and shoveled sidewalks; if someone needed help with a car, there was always somebody in that house who knew what to do. As people moved out to get on with their lives, we all wished them well.

Downtown was only a couple of blocks away so I could walk to Lucas Candies for some homemade chocolate—still some of the best I've ever tasted. The bodegas offered fresh vegetables and herbs and spices we couldn't get in the grocery store, and Vito and Mike's had about the best New York pizza you could ever ask for.

The Hudson River was just a few steps from downtown, although the shoreline had yet to be cleaned up when we moved into the house.

In all, Haverstraw was a wonderful place to live, a small village in the middle of the New York megalopolis.

Chapter 8

Michael was fifteen when I caught him with a cigarette. It had only been a few months since his hero, my father, had died from emphysema after smoking for fifty years.

Michael had watched my father sicken and die over the course of ten years. As it turns out, he had kept his mouth shut when he and my father went fishing and my father had smoked. I don't think they smoked together because my father would have ratted him out, even if it meant exposing his own smoking.

We all knew Daddy was smoking, anyway. If you walked around to the side of the house where his man-cave window was, you'd see a pile of butts. I can imagine him hanging out the window so the smell of smoke wouldn't incriminate him. It wasn't like the odor didn't already permeate the house. All four of his daughters smoked, as did several of the Phippses.

My father started smoking in the 1940s, when cigarette manufacturers were still hiding the dangers of addiction to nicotine. In his high school yearbook, someone had written, "It isn't the cough that carries you off; it's the coffin they carry you off in." Funny little ditty, I thought.

By the sixties, when my sisters and I started smoking, the dangers were known, but the tobacco companies were still denying them and targeting teenagers in their advertising. We fell for it.

Michael watched as my father found breathing increasingly difficult, as he was hospitalized with ever-shorter intervals between stays because of congestion around his heart. When his grandpa was in the hospital, Michael held the position of authority in his chair at the head of the table.

By the time Michael was twelve, my father was using oxygen, which was tethered much of the day to a machine that kept him breathing. The two of them spent a lot of time together, telling silly jokes, talking about fishing and the "olden days." When Shannon was around, they were a threesome.

During the time between when we moved to New York and when my father died, Michael started about one in five sentences with, "Grandpa thinks . . ." or "Grandpa says . . ."

Michael tried to pattern his thinking and attitudes after his grandfather's. He certainly had the same generous spirit. When he heard about a homeless family with six children living in a tent, he packed up his treasured GI Joe collection and brought it to them.

"I'm thirteen," he said. "I'm too old for GI Joe now."

Although the kids at school didn't "get" Michael, my father did, and that meant the world to him. He knew I accepted him, but I was his mother so I had to. From my father, acceptance was a precious gift.

Three weeks before my father died, he sat Michael and Shannon down to talk to them.

"You know, I'm going to die soon," he said.

The two teenagers protested that they didn't want to talk about that.

"Well, I'll still die soon anyway," my father said. "And I want to have the chance to tell you a couple of things."

The kids relented.

"I wish I could have lived a longer life," he said. "That's not going to happen, though. But you should know that I've had a good time. I've laughed every day—a good belly laugh. It's important to do that, no matter what else is happening."

He told them he didn't want them to grieve his death but to celebrate his life.

Three weeks later, he died. He was sixty-seven.

It was a Monday morning, January 8, 1990, and I had to go pick up Michael at school. He was summoned to the office, likely wondering what he was in trouble for this time. As soon as he saw me there, he knew what was wrong.

"Grandpa," he said. "Grandpa died."

Neither of us said much on the way to Massachusetts—a three and a half hour drive—until we were in Rhode Island.

"I don't feel like celebrating," he said.

"I don't either," I answered, and we cried.

That night, with the family around the table, my stepsister, Sally, said. "Remember how much he loved chocolate? I always stole pieces of it now and then, and I replaced it at Christmas." ·

We all did that. As we went around the table we realized he had gotten at least seven pounds of chocolate just three weeks earlier. He couldn't have eaten that much in such a short time. In a few moments, we were scrambling toward all his hiding places.

My stepmother arranged the chocolates lovingly on her biggest platter, held it up high over the table and said, "Lester, you're gonna share."

The rest of the evening was spent devouring the chocolates and telling stories. Michael was beginning to understand what it meant to celebrate a life.

During the next few days, the house was full of family and friends. My friend—Steve Zurier, a former colleague who had moved to Massachusetts the year before—stopped in to spend some time "sitting shiva," as he called it.

I had sat shiva with Jewish friends before. It's a wonderful tradition that keeps the bereaved family comforted for a week after a death.

Steve was right, even though my family isn't Jewish. Between my father's death and his memorial service five days later, the house was never empty. Michael and I retreated into my father's office late at night to go through old photos, which he kept stuffed in drawers of an old dresser and boxes piled in the closet. Being among his things was comforting for both of us, and for Danny, who had arrived the day after Daddy died.

Danny was upset that his grandfather was being cremated instead of buried, and he didn't want to sit near anyone during the memorial service. Change was never easy for him, and the death of someone he loved was more change than he could handle.

The memorial service was held on Friday, and the church was packed to the rafters. Because he had been a newspaper reporter and sports writer for so many years, he was well known; because he had been such a good human being with a marvelous sense of humor, he was well loved. We had received telegrams from Senator Ted Kennedy, from US members of Congress, governors and former governors, plus resolutions from the legislatures of both Massachusetts and Rhode Island.

I read a column I had written for Father's Day two years before. I had surprised him by having it published in the *Providence Journal*—his newspaper.

My sister, Ellen, who hated speaking in public, read a beautiful tribute that ended with, "He gave us so much during his life, and no one can take that away. The only thing we can't have now is new memories of Les Boyd."

A member of his fishing club got up and announced that when the club took boys from an orphanage in Providence fishing each year in June, the day would be known hereafter as Les Boyd Kids' Day.

Then things got silly. Speaker after speaker talked about his practical jokes, and the church was filled with laughter.

A colleague related how an editor loved to have the flag flying outside the door of the bureau's office. There was a small hole drilled in the concrete for the flag and if the first person to enter the building didn't put out the flag, this editor pitched a hissy fit.

It's not that Daddy wasn't patriotic—he definitely was—but he hated how much this editor carried on about having the flag outside every morning. So, one night, he poured cement into the hole in the sidewalk and then made sure he was there, shrouded in cigarette smoke and working on a crossword puzzle, before the editor came in the next morning.

The editor did just what Daddy expected; he got the flag, stalked out the door, cursing and complaining and slammed the flagpole into the cement. My father never moved as the editor cursed and carried on, blaming the city for filling in the hole as he chipped out the cement.

Daddy once put a dead fish under the hubcap of a friend's new car. As the friend tried to identify the stench, my father offered advice.

"Maybe it's something in the upholstery," he said. "Or maybe there's something in the engine. Does it smell like something burning?"

The car dealership got involved, but before they could identify the source, the odor disappeared. Months later, when his friend got a flat tire and took the hubcap off, he saw the fish skeleton. All he could do was laugh, and then seek revenge.

As the stories continued, Michael leaned over to me and whispered, "I get it now."

After the service, Danny agreed that his grandfather knew how to make an exit.

A month or so after my father died, Michael told me he was afraid to cry.

"If I start I'll never stop," he said.

I promised him he would be able to stop.

The next day I got a call at work. It was Rob, calling to tell me that Mike had come home from school in tears two hours before and was still crying. I had Rob put him on.

"See?" he sobbed. "I told you I'd never stop. I told you."

"Do you want me to come home?"

"Yeeeessssss!" he wailed.

In the twenty minutes it took me to get home, he had calmed down a bit, but his eyes were red and swollen and he was still sobbing, gasping those deep, wracking sobs that make a mother feel like hell.

We talked about how empty the world felt without my father, and how we were going to manage without him.

"I talk to him sometimes," Michael said. "Is that bad?"

No, I assured him. I talked to him, too.

We finally decided Michael needed a photo for his bedside table, so he picked one of his favorites—a black and white photo where Daddy was wearing his fishing hat and grinning, his arm thrown up on the edge of his fifteen-foot boat, *Assignment*. I picked a similar one with the same hat and the same grin. We pulled the two pictures out of the album and bought frames for them.

"At least now I won't feel crazy when I say good night to him," Michael said.

That Easter, we decided to spend the weekend at Provincetown on Cape Cod. So Michael and Shannon, my stepmother, my friend—Nancy Cacioppo—and I shared a hotel room. Nancy and I, who worked together, were known as Muffy and Buffy for our pronunciation of "aunt," which our New York colleagues always pronounced "ant."

The joke expanded that weekend to re-name Shannon as Bunny and my stepmother as Grandmama. As we were laughing, Michael interjected, "Well, then, aren't I a Chip off the old Skip?"

We decided to do a whale watch on Easter morning, April 16. It was cold, but clear.

"I'll know Grandpa's soul is at peace if we see whales," Michael said as the boat set out.

We traveled for two hours and saw porpoises, but no whales. I was beginning to lose hope as I watched Michael become increasingly upset.

Suddenly, the boat slowed. Three whales were nearby, and they were approaching the boat.

"They just got back into northern waters," the guide said. "They haven't seen us in months, so they'll probably be pretty curious."

They swam to the boat, and one by one, they rose out of the water to get a closer look. We were no more than ten to twelve feet away from them.

A friend had told me once that looking a whale in the eye changed his perception of the whales forever, and I knew what he meant—there was intelligence and emotion. Those eyes understood more than I had ever imagined, and Michael was having a conversation with one, telling him about his grandfather and how he loved the ocean.

We continued on after fifteen or twenty minutes and came across more whales, which also came close to the boat. It was here that we learned that about one of every four whales has atrociously bad breath. The stench brought tears to our eyes.

"Don't tell him his breath is bad," Michael joked to me. "The poor thing can't help it."

The trip was filled with incredibly silly behavior, including our singing at the drop of a hat. One of us would drop a hat and we all broke into "Springtime for Hitler," the tune from Mel Brooks' comedy, *The Producers*.

But at dinner during the night of the whale watch, Michael was less eager to participate when a family with a pretty teenage girl sat at the table next to ours, and she started making eyes at him.

"Stop it!" he hissed at us. "She won't like me if you keep acting like that!"

Unfortunately, it was a romance that was doomed from the start. We kept acting up and eventually he had to join in. If our behavior bothered her, the romance wouldn't have worked out anyway.

The year my father died, we learned things he had never intended us to know. It would have ruined his reputation as a curmudgeon if we had known he started the *Letters to Santa* project in my hometown, and that as each of his children turned eighteen, he stopped giving us big Christmas gifts and spent that money on another family's Christmas.

We decided we would adopt a family. We wanted one with two little boys because when I first became a single mom, my father made sure my boys got gifts from Santa.

"Buy something for yourself, too," Daddy had said to me. "The kids will notice if Santa doesn't leave you anything."

That first Christmas, we pulled a family from the notebook at People to People, a nonprofit serving Rockland County, New York. We bought simple gifts for the boys—new toys and clothes—and a warm sweater for the mom.

On Christmas morning, Michael burst into tears as we were opening our presents.

"What's wrong?" I asked. I thought it might be that this was our first Christmas without my father.

"Oh, nothing," he sobbed. "It's just that somewhere there are two little boys who still believe in Santa because of us and I love that."

My father's death left Michael feeling alone and outcast again. He began to increase his use of alcohol and drugs to ease the pain.

I did my best to introduce Michael to the finer things in life, including good comedy. We watched a lot of W. C. Fields, Marx Brothers, Laurel and Hardy, and Mel Brooks while the boys were kids. In fact, Mel Brooks' *The Producers* was our favorite movie. We could watch it over and over, reciting the dialogue and singing along with "Springtime for Hitler."

A few months after my father died, we were both in the mood for a good comedy, so we went to the video store. Michael kept pulling out sophomoric *Police Academy* movies as I tried to explain that we both already knew all the jokes in those movies and we needed something a little more witty and creative. I pulled out *Monty Python and the Holy Grail*, and Michael scowled.

"It's my money," I said as I paid for it.

Michael moped all the way home and slouched down onto the sofa.

Within a few minutes, though, he was laughing hysterically. He had a new favorite movie. When it was over, he rewound the tape and took it upstairs to watch again. He watched it over and over all night long and again the next afternoon and evening.

He started watching old Monty Python episodes on PBS and memorizing his favorite sketches, including "Dead Parrot" and the "Lumberjack Song." Later, "Always Look on the Bright Side of Life," from the movie, *Life of Brian*, became his favorite.

#

I didn't like the kids he was hanging around with and I did my best to keep him away from them, but he had gotten a job and he was going to hang around with the people he chose. They were at school; they came into the Burger King where he worked; and Kevin was still in his Boy Scout troop.

People tried to steer him straight. His Scout leaders did their best to keep him occupied and working on advancing through the ranks.

Russ Karkheck talked sense at him.

"Inside, he's a great kid. Don't lose sight of that," Russ said.

Our neighbors, Charlie and Kathy Frey, worked to try and hold Michael together. They moved into the neighborhood when Michael was fifteen.

"Mom," Michael said excitedly one Saturday afternoon. "The new neighbors are moving in! The guy has a ponytail and he rides motorcycles and he plays guitar!"

I was a little worried about the new neighbors and how they would affect my peace and quiet, until I met them.

Charlie rebuilt old American motorcycles and played blues guitar. He became Michael's mentor and was the only person aside from Rob and me who could get away with calling him Mikey. Everyone else called him Mike. Although for the most part, I continued to call him Michael.

"Hey, Mikey, did you feed the cats?" Charlie would holler if Rob and I weren't home at dinnertime.

"Hey, Mikey, wanna ride in the sidecar? I need ballast!"

Charlie taught Michael how to play guitar and gave him an appreciation for the blues. It was a trip to watch the two of them listening to good blues albums.

In Michael's senior year of high school, I found pot seeds in his room and confronted him. Yes, he had smoked, but so had everyone from my generation and they seemed to be doing fine.

Because of the generation I came from, I believed pot was safer than booze. I believed it wasn't addictive. I wasn't terribly worried about it, although I told him I disapproved and expected him to lay off.

Like many from my generation, I felt like a hypocrite.

When he was seventeen, Michael started working at Danielle's restaurant, Rick's Club American. She and her siblings had sold Dubonnay's and opened Rick's, which became a successful family restaurant and bar. Michael was working as a line cook and doing well at the job.

He didn't do so well at school, bringing home barely passing grades, skipping homework assignments, and not studying. Still, he was acing most of his tests, so his teachers weren't inclined to fail him.

Chapter 9

Mike graduated high school with a quarter point to spare. We weren't certain he would actually graduate until three weeks before, when his final grades were processed and we could breathe a sigh of relief.

Hazen had said he wouldn't be able to come to the graduation because the paper mill where he worked was on shut-down and he couldn't get away. In the days before graduation, Michael tried repeatedly to call his father but got no answer.

"This isn't right," he said. "These are people of habit. I mean, they come home at six, eat supper, watch TV, and go to bed at eleven. There are no deviations."

Mike finally called Danny, who told him the reason no one was picking up the phone: Hazen was on vacation.

Mike was crushed.

"I would have understood if he had just told us he was going to be on vacation," Mike said. "I know we weren't sure until three weeks ago, but he could have told me the truth."

Hazen probably had forgotten the date of the graduation—schools in Georgia let out three to four weeks before those in New York—and didn't want Mike's feelings to be hurt.

Charlie was quick to come up with an idea that would cheer Mike up. He had just finished restoring a red and white Indian motorcycle—the school colors of North Rockland High School. Charlie thought it would be cool for Mike to be chauffeured to graduation on the bike.

Meanwhile, my stepmother had made plans to surprise Mike by showing up the morning of his graduation.

The day was perfect and Mike was over being hurt by his father's absence.

In nearly every photo I have of my son that day, his red mortarboard is duct taped to a white motorcycle helmet. On the way to the school for the graduation ceremony, Mike gave the "princess wave" as cars honked and people hollered their congratulations. He was the center of attention and he loved it. When he got to the school, he stepped off the bike, ripped off the duct tape, handed the helmet to Charlie, and walked into the school without a word.

I arrived a moment later and stopped to help a girl who was having trouble with her collar.

"Whose mom are you?" she asked.

"Well, did you see the guy who just arrived on the motorcycle?"

"Ohmygod! That was *so COO-WELLL!*"

Mike's graduation gift was my old car, a five-year-old Chevy Nova. It was in good shape and it ran well, and it would get him back and forth to work. In the fall, it would make it easy for him to get to school; he was enrolled in the culinary arts program at Rockland Community College.

It only took him three weeks to run it into a tree.

"I broke my new toy," he said.

"Not funny. Now you have to pay to fix it because it's your responsibility."

The damage was repairable, and Charlie knew someone who would do it cheaply, so he paid $700 to have it fixed.

Still, I was furious that he could be so careless.

"I wouldn't worry about it," the newspaper's executive editor said to me. "To a boy, a car is something you ruin and replace. You just buy another cheap one because they grow on trees."

The summer after graduation, Mike went to Georgia as usual. He had drug and alcohol connections there, and the substance abuse only made him bitter and angry over his life. He had birth defects; he had learning disabilities; his father didn't know how to deal with him. He was angry at Danny for having everything he wanted—athletic ability, popularity, a girlfriend who adored him, and his father's approval. He compensated by self-medicating.

The rest of us were in denial about Mike's alcohol and drug use. Sure, he was using some, but didn't we all at his age?

By mid-1992, Danny had a daughter, Lauren—the result of a brief high school affair. The paternity test hadn't been done yet, but Mike went to visit her anyway. I had gotten a photo in the mail from her mother, and Lauren was a dead ringer for me. I was a grandmother at age thirty-nine.

"I got to hold her and feed her," Mike told me. "She's beautiful."

Danny was upset, but before long, Danny claimed Lauren and she became part of his family. She is an adventurous young woman, unafraid of new experiences.

In August, we found out Jennifer was pregnant. She and Danny were married in a small ceremony. They had planned to be married a year later, but the pregnancy forced them to move up the date. Peyton was born in February 1993, followed by Meghan in December 1996, and Trey in March 2000.

Mike came home and started the culinary arts program. I wasn't about to give up hope that he would quit screwing around and settle down.

He started dating Beth, a young woman he met at a poetry reading, and they seemed to be good for each other. She was a freshman at Vassar, an hour north of Haverstraw, and her parents lived in Rockland County, so they were together most weekends. He seemed to be taking better care of himself and settling in at college.

That fall, Mike had his first kidney infection.

The urologist who cared for him wouldn't believe it was the first time. "He must have had infections," he said.

People who have the urine diversion that Mike had usually are plagued by kidney infections because once the ureters are implanted into the sigmoid colon, the renal system, which is sterile, is subjected to bacteria from the colon. But a review of Mike's medical records showed no sign of kidney infections. He had been unusually healthy for someone with this diversion.

Still, there was no warning that Mike was more vulnerable to colon cancer than other people, or that the diversion should be reversed. I'm sure we all would have preferred an ostomy bag to cancer, but when he was released from the hospital, still on our insurance plan, we had no clue that he was in danger from anything but kidney infections.

Mike turned nineteen in November, but as long as he was in school, he could stay on our insurance plan, at least until he turned twenty-one. We didn't know then that he would be deemed uninsurable because of his birth defect, or that he had a one in four chance of developing colon cancer. We didn't know that most restaurants don't offer their employees health benefits.

We were blissfully unaware of what lay ahead.

One night in February, Mike didn't come home from work. By now he was working at a grocery store and it closed at ten o'clock. He was usually home before midnight, but as the night dragged on, I knew something was different about this night. He wasn't coming home.

The next day, I called some of his friends. No one knew where he was. Although I had quit smoking four and a half years before, I begged a cigarette from a friend. I called the hospitals to see if he was there, but he wasn't. I smoked another couple of cigarettes.

One of his friends agreed to meet me at the house at four o'clock that afternoon, even though he didn't know where Mike was.

"We can plan a strategy to find him," Christian said. "We can call Bobsey. He might know something."

When I got home at four, I found a note on the refrigerator. Mike had lost his job. He had flunked out of community college—I didn't know that was possible. He wanted to disappear because he couldn't face me. He wasn't worth saving, he wrote. He thought I should just give up on him.

Christian and Bobsey set out to find him. I called Danielle. Her daughter, Colette, attended the community college; maybe she had seen or heard something.

Colette was reluctant to talk to me because every time she had seen Mike in recent months, he was high. She hated to be the one to tell me.

Finally, Beth told me they had broken up and Mike was seeing someone else—a young woman who had threatened her if she ever spoke to Mike again.

I went and bought a pack of cigarettes.

I met the young woman the next day when Mike listened to his friends and reappeared. He wanted to be on his own now, since he and G were going to get married.

"You can't get a job first?" I asked. "If you love each other, waiting a couple months won't hurt."

G wanted to get married and then move in with us; Rob and I said no. We knew it would be trouble. It was time for tough love.

Two days later, they showed up again, married.

"We eloped," she said, gloating. Mike looked uncomfortable.

She still wanted us to let them move in. Instead I bought them a tent and sleeping bags. I wanted to help them, but there was no way she was moving into my house.

"You're an adult now," I said. "You're on your own."

They stayed in our backyard for a couple of weeks, but Mike was drinking heavily, and from what Charlie and Kathy heard, so was G. They fought whenever they drank, and they drank almost every day. She was jealous of everyone, and although Mike had found another job, he was calling in sick because of hangovers.

Finally, Rob told them they had to leave. I couldn't face Mike and kick him out once and for all.

Now they were camping in the woods. They could be arrested for trespassing if they were discovered. Like most places, being homeless was a crime in Rockland County, New York.

A couple of weeks later, three police cars with six officers from the next town over appeared at my door. They wanted to know where Mike was. A former cop's fiancée's purse had been stolen and they suspected Mike and G.

"He's grown and on his own," I said, "and you're violating the law coming outside your jurisdiction over a purse theft."

I called the town supervisor the next day to complain. Later that afternoon, as I was outside working in my garden, a man came into my yard.

"I'm looking for Mike," he said. "I got business with him. He stole my girlfriend's purse and she had a diamond bracelet worth $10,000 in there."

"I don't know where he is," I said. And it was true.

"I think you do." It sounded threatening, but neighbors were outside and I knew he wouldn't hurt me with them watching.

I faced him.

"Get off my property. Now." I spoke softly but firmly and stood my ground. "I'll call the Haverstraw cops. They do have jurisdiction here and they're not your buddies."

He backed off.

Turns out he was a former cop who had been thrown off the force because of a drug conviction. His buddies on the force had come out to the house the night before and gotten a talking-to for going outside of their jurisdiction, especially since the person they were trying to intimidate was a newspaper reporter.

I had no more trouble with them, but Mike and G were arrested.

I got the call while I was at work and my friend, Andy Chabra, was standing nearby. I burst into tears after I refused to post bail and hung up. Andy, one of my oldest and best friends put his arms around me and let me get his shirt all teary and snotty. He kept assuring me that Mike would be OK eventually. But I was beginning to doubt it.

Later that night, a colleague called to tell me the report was going into the police briefs section the next day, just so I would be prepared. "I wish I could keep it out," she said.

"You can't," I replied.

G's parents bailed them out, and since there was no evidence, they never were convicted. I'm convinced that had they not been Caucasian and well-cleaned up for their court date, they would have been in a lot more trouble.

A few days later, the Department of Social Services called me. Mike and G had come in for help and the social worker wanted to know if they could live with me. Like G's parents, I said no.

They were put up in a motel for a few days until they found a small, cheap apartment. Mike's friend, Dave, had found a job for G—if she didn't mind cleaning rooms in the hotel where he worked. I bought them a bunch of kitchen stuff as a wedding present, hoping this might be a turning point that would set them on their feet.

I tried to be a friend to G. If Mike loved her, she must have redeeming qualities. They started coming to church with me and things appeared to stabilize for a while, but G lost her job and they lost the apartment. They moved in with G's parents, and she found a job in a small bakery.

G loved the bakery and her work there. Mike was working at a restaurant and reporting to work every day. Again, I had hopes that they would get on their feet.

Then the bakery closed.

Chapter 10

Mike and G decided to make a fresh start by moving to Georgia, near Mike's dad and Danny and his family. Mike could get a job with a decent restaurant and they could live more cheaply in Brunswick, Georgia, than in New York.

I was scared of having Mike so far away. It was one thing to have him visit his father for a few weeks in the summer, but another thing entirely to have him move there permanently. But I knew he needed this fresh start and I knew he would be able to afford to rent a small place and be on his own whether G was able to find a job or not.

The night they arrived in Georgia, Danny called me, furious at what G said I had told her about Jennifer's family. According to G, I had described them as country hicks.

It had never happened. She told them a pack of lies, and when I got Mike on the phone, she was standing next to him, so he didn't say anything. Danny told me later that Mike seemed afraid to stand up to her, and she had a smug look on her face the entire time. That's what made him realize I was telling the truth.

Mike found a job in the kitchen of a fine-dining restaurant on St. Simons Island, and they rented a two-bedroom mobile home about twenty minutes outside of Brunswick. Things seemed stable, but I was hundreds of miles away. Danny said the kids loved G and looked forward to playing with her whenever she and Mike came by. They seemed to be getting onto their feet.

But G was spending money they didn't have. Mike came home one afternoon to find she had bought a Shop-Vac. Another afternoon, she had downed an entire bottle of single malt Scotch. Later Danny told me Mike and G were fighting constantly.

I didn't know that Mike attempted suicide during this time until years later.

Finally, G decided to go home to her parents' house for a few weeks. Danny hoped the move would be permanent, but she came back and things picked up where they left off.

Eventually, they couldn't pay the rent so they sneaked out in the middle of the night, leaving most of their belongings, and headed for her parents' house. Their car broke down somewhere in Virginia and G's parents called and asked if I would give them my credit card number. I refused. There was no way I was going to let them have access to my credit card when they were acting so irresponsibly.

They got back to New York and moved back in with G's parents. I don't know a lot of what happened there and I don't want to. Some rocks are better left unturned.

They weren't back in town long when G's family suggested that she and Mike move to Florida to care for an elderly relative whose health was failing. Once again, they packed up the car and drove south, and again, I was left not knowing what was happening in Mike's life. I still had hopes he would turn his life around, although just about everyone else had given up on him.

G complained that her charge was fussy and cranky most of the time, but they got along well enough for her to stay. Mike got another restaurant job in Fort Lauderdale and they settled in.

Back North, Rob's mother, Elsie, was sick and getting sicker. She had been diagnosed with breast cancer six years prior and had surgery. An X-ray a few months earlier had shown a tiny spot on her lung, but there was no firm diagnosis. She decided not to have the spot biopsied because she was too old for the aggressive treatment that would be required if it was cancer.

But one day she had trouble breathing and was taken to the emergency room. A couple of days later, the news came: she had cancer throughout her body.

When we told her, she sobbed for a minute. She then dried her eyes and said that not many members of her family had made it to eighty and she figured she should be grateful for that. Together, we decided that she would go home and we would call hospice to help care for her. No chemo, no radiation.

The orthopedist who was called in to look at the bone X-rays suggested we try radiation, but we refused.

"But you can't do nothing," he said, obviously disturbed that we would "give up."

"We're not doing nothing," Rob said. "We're going to keep her comfortable and help her enjoy her final days."

Danny and Mike decided to come up and see her before she died. Mike would drive as far as Brunswick and then the two of them would travel together to my house.

G's car was broken down and she wanted Danny and Mike to tow it to New York so her father could fix it. But Danny drove a small Nissan and it wouldn't tow a full-sized car that distance.

G let loose with a tirade that shocked Danny.

"I was in the Marines and I've never heard anything like that," he told me.

He still refused.

As they drove, they stopped every few hours and Mike would call G. They drove straight through—sixteen hours—and when they got to the house, Danny called Jennifer and the kids to let them know he had arrived safely. They talked for a few minutes and then hung up so Mike could call G. When he mentioned to G that Danny had called Jennifer already, we could hear G's screaming from the next room. Mike apologized to her again and again as she ranted.

We went to see Elsie the next day and Danny decided to ride in the ambulance with her on the way home.

Elsie had wanted to stop before she left the hospital and see her brother-in-law, Rob's Uncle Mick, who was there with a broken pelvis. He was her sister's husband and the two couples had lived together most of their adult lives. When Rob's father died fourteen years earlier, Uncle Mick had promised to look after Elsie. This would be their last chance to see each other. The attendants said they didn't have time.

As they went outside into the chill winter air, Danny pulled up the blanket to her chin. One of the attendants told him not to touch her.

"This is my grandmother," Danny said. "I will touch her when I please. I will adjust her covers; I will hold her hand and I won't hear another word from you. What do you think you're carrying here, a pizza?"

Danny lodged a complaint with hospice, but I don't know whether or not the attendants were disciplined.

When we got Elsie home, she wept with joy. This was where she wanted to be.

We spent the day at the house waiting for the live-in attendant to arrive, and when she did, Elsie was frightened. She was a tall African woman with a distinct accent. Here was Elsie, an elderly, frail woman with a fifth-grade education, being left alone with a stranger from a foreign country.

But within a day or two, Elsie and the woman had become fast friends. Elsie believed God had sent her this woman to allay her fears, and Danny and Mike felt better about going home.

Hospice workers and family surrounded Elsie. A week or so before she died, another woman came to care for her—an African American woman whose husband was a Baptist preacher. He came by every day to pray with her and she was grateful, even though she had been a lifelong Catholic.

We came by with our dog, a cocker spaniel named Zoe, who Elsie insisted was her best friend. We put Zoe on the bed with her and the two of them napped together.

But as the weeks wore on, Elsie got weaker. She slept most of the day and enjoyed listening to her new preacher friend as he read the Bible and prayed with her. She had stopped eating, and finally a hospice worker told Rob he needed to tell her it was OK for her to go. She was fighting because she was worried about whether he would be OK, and he needed to assure her that he would.

"You know, Mom, I know how much you want to see Dad again," he said, fighting his tears. "Ron and I will be fine. You took good care of us and now we're OK on our own. It's time for you to be with Dad. I love you."

He got through it without crying, and Elsie died a couple of days later, peacefully and free of pain. Five days later, Uncle Mick died, content at having kept his promise to care for Elsie.

Again, Danny and Mike would come home, but this time, Mike would stay.

All the way back to Georgia after the first trip, Danny talked to Mike as though it was a deprogramming session. "You deserve better than this," he said. "You deserve to be treated like a human being."

As soon as Mike was back in Florida, he decided Danny was right. When Elsie died, Mike came home with his few belongings and with permission from us to stay at the house for up to three months while he looked for work and an apartment.

Finally, I thought, this was the beginning of his new life. He was going to get it together.

It only took a couple of days for Mike to find a job, and he fell in with his old friends. He seemed to be doing OK, working and socializing with friends. He started divorce proceedings, which made all of us happy. He and G were just bad for each other and nothing was going to change that.

I was happy to have Mike nearby again, although I was still in denial about his addictions. He was getting to work on time and that was what mattered.

If he was an addict, he wouldn't be able to handle a job—right?

Chapter 11

On April 14, 1997, I was reading my devotional at bedtime, as usual. I had two books, and both were using the 23rd Psalm as the passage of the day. In all the time I had been reading from both devotionals, they never had the same passage on the same day.

As I read the verse, "Yea, though I walk through the valley of the shadow of death, I will fear no evil, for thou art with me," I felt a chill. I couldn't shake the feeling that Mike was in that valley as I was reading.

I tried to tell myself it was illogical, but the feeling persisted. I didn't sleep much that night; I lay awake, praying that Mike would make it through the valley.

I was distracted at work the next day. I hadn't seen Mike in the morning and I wanted to talk to him. He was out by the time I got home. He had said he wanted to get together with his friend, Bobsey, and do his taxes. He was getting a refund and he planned to celebrate.

That evening, I assumed he was with Bobsey, but Bobsey came by at about ten, looking sick and scared.

"I don't know where Mike is," he said. "He's in bad shape. He had a lot to drink and he's depressed. I'm scared." Bobsey decided he would go out driving and try to find Mike and I would stay at the house in case there was news. I was frantic. I had no idea what to do other than pray.

Mike was out on the street somewhere, if he was still alive.

#

The sound of his heart filled his ears.

He'd fix that soon.

He stopped in the middle of the bridge and looked down.

About thirty feet, he figured. Good. Below him was a concrete ledge jutting out maybe ten feet above the water.

He could almost hear his body thud against it and he wondered if that was what would kill him.

Maybe it would just knock him unconscious so he wouldn't panic as the murky water filled his lungs and carried him off to peace.

I'm twenty-two, and all I've done is fail. Just a huge disappointment to everybody who ever loved me. My friends are getting sick of hearing about it.

Mom keeps hoping, and I keep letting her down. I can't believe she still thinks I'll do something with my life. I don't know if it's optimism or blind stupidity. Rob hasn't convinced her yet that I'm useless. I'm not going anywhere.

And Dad, Jesus, Dad. Does he even have a clue? He's so wrapped up in his life with Linda and Scott. I don't think he even thinks about me except to wish I'd disappear.

G, she'll just be happy to hear I'm gone. Maybe nobody will tell her. She'll call one day and Mom will say, "Didn't you hear? He's dead. You killed him." Mom will blame her. She can't believe it's all my fault and she can't fix it. She always thinks she can fix it.

Bobsey's out looking for me. He knows. I drank way more than usual tonight. The hard stuff, too. I probably pissed him off but good. God, I'm a lousy drunk. You'd think by now I'd be good at it. I've been doing it long enough.

His heart was still pounding as he leaned over the rail.

A little more . . . a little more and it'll all be over. They'll find me in the morning somewhere downstream. Maybe I'll float all the way out to the Hudson before they find me.

Suddenly, he stood upright, as though a hand had pulled him back from the edge. He started running.

\#

It was midnight when the phone rang. I don't remember the officer's name, but the first thing he said after his name was, "Your son is OK."

Mike had run all the way from the bridge in Stony Point to the police station and asked to be brought to the hospital. He was afraid he would kill himself and he didn't want to die, he had told them. I would be able to see him in the morning.

April 16 was Mike's first day without alcohol or drugs in several years.

I drove to the hospital and went to the ward where he was. It was a locked psychiatric ward; I had visited other people on these wards before. I had taken a career course in high school that involved volunteering at a state hospital, where people stood in lines as they awaited the medication that would quiet the voices in their heads or keep them from wanting to hurt themselves. The medicines dulled the pain of psychiatric illnesses, but they didn't cure.

But my child was on this ward now. He was standing inside the door as I was let in, holding his flannel shirt and a book. I had brought him cigarettes and he handed several out to people who had given him one during the day. He had to wait for an attendant to come light his cigarette.

"We're not allowed to have matches," he said.

He had to carry his belongings with him because if he put something down, someone would pick it up and walk away with it.

He asked me to bring him some soda the next time I came in.

"But no glass. They don't allow glass in here," he said. "And bring it in a paper bag, not plastic.

It reminded me of Arlo Guthrie's "Alice's Restaurant," when Officer Obie put Arlo in jail and took away his belt so he wouldn't hang himself, and the toilet seat so he wouldn't hit himself in the head and drown in the toilet, and finally, the toilet paper so he wouldn't unroll it out the window and escape.

Mike laughed at that. "Alice's Restaurant" was a Thanksgiving tradition at our house, along with a viewing of *King Kong* after dinner.

He looked as though a weight had been lifted from him. He was getting the help he needed even though he didn't have health insurance. Medicaid would cover his hospitalization.

The psychiatrist diagnosed him with depression and addiction and prescribed rehab at a hospital in Orangetown. The clinic was well respected, but I was still in denial. That's when Mike called me Cleopatra, Queen of Denial.

I learned a lot in the next few weeks, about me, about addiction, about who my friends were.

Once Mike was in rehab, the only time we could see him was from eleven to one on Sundays, and only if we attended an educational session at ten. We also chose to attend Al-Anon meetings before the educational sessions.

Al-Anon was helpful, but it seemed many of the people there were as addicted to the meetings and the jargon as their loved ones were to drugs and alcohol. I suppose if Mike had fallen back into addiction, I would have been more appreciative of Al-Anon. But Mike would be one of the 30 percent of people who only need to go through rehab once. There were parents at the meeting whose children were in for their third or fourth time.

I heard things about people I knew that surprised me. One woman reminded me about the confidentially, and I smiled and said, "I don't know who you are."

"Yes you do," she insisted.

I put my arm around her shoulder. "Never saw you before," I said.

I read a lot about the Twelve Steps and Alcoholics Anonymous. I wanted to understand what Mike would be going through as he worked the steps on his way to wellness. I finally understood that I hadn't caused his addiction and I couldn't cure it; that had to come from him.

Mike took it seriously. He worked hard at understanding why he did the drugs and alcohol. He saw it as a chronic, progressive illness that he could control if he kept at it; otherwise, it would control him. He would never be cured; he would be in recovery. People with diabetes have to take insulin and be very conscious of what they eat; addicts have to be aware of their triggers and not use.

Disease management.

On our first Sunday, Mike and Rob talked about their relationship. Rob was more of a father to him in many ways than his own father; Mike was a son to Rob. It was the first time they had really talked about their feelings toward one another.

As the weeks wore on, I saw my son returning to me. The happy kid was coming out again, being silly and cracking inappropriate jokes.

I had missed church for four weeks when I went to a consistory meeting (I was an elder, a senior member of the church's governing board), only to be told by a fellow board member that I needed to be seen in church on Sundays.

It was bad enough that no one from church except the pastor had called me to see how we were doing—even though they should have known what was going on because of prayer requests on Sunday and in the church newsletter.

"I have one time a week I can see my son and that is Sunday mornings," I told her. "Given the choice between seeing my son, who loves me, and putting in an appearance at church so you won't gossip or criticize me, I'll choose seeing my son."

She apologized, saying she forgot my son was in rehab; I was upset that she hadn't asked if everything was OK, considering my decade-long record of being in church just about every Sunday, of being in the choir and teaching Sunday school, chairing the worship committee, being on the youth and music committees, and being on the board for eight years. After all the support I had given the church, I had hoped for a little more support when I needed it. I felt very much on my own.

Mike's divorce papers came while he was in rehab and he signed them. That would be the end of it. G was in Florida and he was in New York. They were done after less than two years, and I felt an overwhelming sense of relief. The marriage had been a disaster and it didn't matter whose fault it was. I imagined Mike was as much to blame for its failure as G; I was just glad it was over.

Once Mike came out of rehab, he would stay in a halfway house for three months. There was one across the street from our house and I thought that would be perfect. I wanted him close to home.

"Mom, I can't do that," he said. "I need to change everything, and that means getting out of Haverstraw."

He chose a program in Schenectady, about two hours upstate, just outside of Albany. Schenectady has the honor of having more halfway houses and mental health homes than anywhere else in New York State. It is the former home of a huge General Electric plant that closed years ago and left a boatload of PCBs in the sediments of the Hudson River. It also is the home of Union College, Rob's alma mater.

It was while Mike was in this program and still on Medicaid that we learned his "plumbing" left him vulnerable to colon cancer and uninsurable. Studies had shown that people with this urine diversion tended to have a much higher risk of developing cancer at the implant sites. Mike needed to get colonoscopies every year. Once the Medicaid stopped, so would the colonoscopies, unless he could find a job with insurance that would cover them. Otherwise, he would need to find a gastroenterologist who would allow him to pay in monthly installments.

Mike moved into a room at the YMCA once he was out of the halfway program. He had a job as a cook and he was doing well.

Rob and I took a day trip to see him and we hardly recognized the clean-cut young man who walked down the steps of the Y.

We drove to Saratoga for lunch, and I ordered an iced tea.

"Mom, you can order a beer if you want," he said. "I'm the alcoholic, not you."

We had iced tea anyway.

We walked around Saratoga and I bought him a porkpie hat at a second-hand store because he thought it would be a good look for him.

On the way back to Schenectady and a promised tour of the Union College campus, Mike started talking about where he had been before he sobered up. "Everybody has their scams to get money," he said. He and G had theirs, too.

He told me they had stolen the purse, although there was no jewelry in it, no matter what the police were told. It had a few dollars in it—enough to buy supper. That was pretty close to as bad as it got for him.

He also started to describe another scam that involved writing a bad check.

Rob was white-knuckled as he drove.

I interrupted Mike. "I have a new rule," I said. "Mike, you can't discuss your felonies with Mommy anymore. That's the rule now."

There are some things Rob and I really don't want to know. I'm just not curious about some aspects of the pre-sobriety life of my son.

The heat and humidity were suffocating, and I'm not a person who enjoys that kind of weather. By the end of the Union College tour, my feet were swollen and blistered and I felt awful. We went to the mall for some air-conditioning.

After spending so many summers in Georgia, Mike and Danny both were pretty much unaffected by the heat. Mike was wearing long pants and shoes and socks, and he couldn't figure out why I was so uncomfortable.

I don't think we were even back to the interstate on the way home when Mike called Danny to tell him about the new rule. With Mike sober and less angry about his life, he and Danny had become closer. They liked nothing better than to find ways to annoy me.

The new rule became a joke.

"Don't tell Mom about that; it involves that felony, remember?"

"I was never charged with anything."

A month or so later, we went to Georgia to visit Danny and Jennifer and the kids. I heard about the new rule once or twice and we laughed about it. Then I bought a cookbook of favorite recipes from St. Simon's Island chefs. As I was paging through it, Danny pointed to one of the chefs.

"Hey, I know that boy," he said. "Me and him blew up a van."

"Pop quiz," I said. "What's the rule?"

Oh, he said, it wasn't a felony because the van belonged to the guy. See, his girlfriend had the keys and wouldn't give them back and the van wasn't running anyway, so they got a bunch of—

"Explosives," I said, cutting him off mid-sentence. "Enough to blow up a van. I'm pretty sure that's not legal."

People think it's funny when I tell them about the rule I had to make, and it is pretty funny; it just isn't a joke.

Chapter 12

A few months after getting out of rehab, Mike rented a room in a large rooming house. It was only a single room, but he was still sober and he was working and paying the rent on time, and he was attending meetings.

One of his high school friends, also named Mike, had moved to Schenectady and Mike was intent on helping Mike P. get past his addictions.

"He won't drag me down, Mom, I promise," Mike told me when I went to visit one day. As I was leaving, Mike P. was walking toward me. He looked awful—thin and pale, weak, his eyes red and watery. As far as Mike knew, Mike P. never did sober up.

But I was worried about all the time Mike was spending around people who were still using or newly sober. Finally, Mike put me at ease.

"Mom, when I got sober, I prayed. I made a promise. I told God that if he would help me to stay sober, I'd chase drunks for the rest of my life."

He was chasing drunks as a means to stay sober and to be an example to people who were just becoming sober. He wasn't offering help where none was wanted. Mike P. had asked him for help, as had others. Mike was there to listen and to help.

He slipped once, a week after his birthday. He bought some beer and had a couple before throwing the rest away. I remember the anguish in his voice as he told me about the beer.

"Well then," I said. "You're back to Day One, and you're not going to drink today."

It was the last time he would touch alcohol.

One of my favorite things to do was to call Mike's home phone and leave silly messages. "Mikey, it's Mommy. I'm just calling to make sure you brushed your teeth this morning."—"It's supposed to rain so I want you to remember your umbrella."—"Are you eating enough red meat?" His friends got as big a charge out of the messages as Mike did.

But about eight months after he got sober, he called and asked me to lay off the messages for a little while. "I met someone and I just want her to meet you before she hears the messages," he said. "Her name is Janet and you're gonna love her." I agreed, and Rob and I decided to go up a couple of weeks later and meet her.

Janet was from Schenectady. Her father was an engineer working for state government. Her parents were divorced and her mother, who also worked for state government, was married to an engineer who did contract work for what was left of General Electric.

Janet was an art student at a two-year college. I'm not sure who introduced the two of them, but it didn't take them long to realize they both had the same twisted sense of humor. She had a pierced eyebrow and a tattoo around her upper arm. Five years earlier I might have looked askance at that, but I knew better by this time.

Janet is tiny—barely five feet tall—and she often shops in the children's section of the consignment shop. Her voice is quiet and sweet. One would think she's a pushover, but she's tough. When that sweet voice says, "Excuse me?" I know enough to step aside.

I think sassy is a great word to describe Janet. Everything about her seemed to complement Mike, so when they decided to share a double room at the place where Mike lived, I was happy.

On our way home after that first meeting, Rob asked if I had noticed the pierced eyebrow. I had. Did he notice the tattoo? He did.

"I like her a lot," I said. He nodded in agreement.

I started leaving messages again.

Mike and Janet got two kittens, Finley, an orange tabby; and Pandora, a gray and tan calico. Within a few months, they were looking for an apartment. They found a tiny place in a Victorian house not far from Union College, a neighborhood with plenty of other young people.

Mike continued to work as a chef and chase drunks. I heard a lot of their stories. One young man had lost a leg to cancer and was trying to get on with his life, hoping the cancer was gone for good.

One weekend, Danielle and I headed north to pay Mike and Janet a visit. He had been honest about the size of the apartment, but it seemed to be big enough for the two of them and the cats. Mike had made guacamole and Janet had baked meringue cookies. We decided we had to run to the store to get some food for supper. Even though the kitchen was tiny, we all wanted to cook.

As soon as we got out of the car, Mike jumped into a shopping cart. "Can I have candy?" he asked.

I decided to play along. "No, and don't touch anything."

As we cruised the aisles of the store, Mike kept reaching out. "Oh, I want that!"

People were staring, but that only encouraged him. Janet kept moving his hands back into the cart and telling him "no" as I pushed the cart through the store. We put vegetables in and he tossed them back. My goofy kid was back, and he was just as stubborn as ever about not growing up.

Mike never was concerned about what other people would think of his actions; in fact, he deliberately acted out to make people either laugh or question his sanity.

Mike talked occasionally about what being a recovering addict meant to him and how it affected his thinking. He wanted to prove to everyone around him that being sober enabled him to have more fun than being drunk.

My stepmother, who had been in recovery for several years before Mike sobered up, dressed up as a clown on weekends. "Some people are too busy being sober to have any fun," she said. "But I have my life back and I'm going to make the best of it."

Mike shared that philosophy. Although my stepmother left her twelve-step group, she found healing and support in her church. "Everybody at AA talks about drinking," she said. "I'm tired of talking about drinking; it just makes me want to drink."

Mike, on the other hand, found healing in his twelve-step group. He needed to "work the steps" to gain strength and insight into what led him to use drugs and alcohol. He used the same methods to work on his depression because he didn't want to take antidepressants for the rest of his life.

This "recovery model" for mental illnesses was just coming into being in the mid-nineties; it has gained wide recognition since. As with addiction, depression has its triggers, and people who have it lose all motivation. In a recovery model, you recognize the symptoms and address them. Instead of staying in bed, you make yourself get up and shower. Exercise is important because it has been shown to reduce symptoms of depression, so no matter how much you don't feel like exercising, you do it.

The recovery model isn't easy because depression is powerful, but Mike was determined not to become dependent on any chemical substance ever again.

The only time Mike took antidepressants again was much later when we discovered his cancer was back and there was no longer a chance of a cure.

"It was so good to see the old Michael," Danielle said as we were driving back along the thruway that night. She agreed that he and Janet seemed good for each other.

The first Christmas they were in the apartment, Mike and Janet bought a huge tree. It stood over seven feet tall and was at least five feet across at the base. It took up half of the tiny living room, and when Mike and Rob went to put it up, it kept falling over. Finally, they tied it to the locks on two of the windows to stabilize it.

We decorated the tree with handmade ornaments—some I had crocheted, some made by Janet. We had nowhere near enough to cover the entire tree, but it was still a wonderful afternoon.

We met Janet's mom and stepfather, Pat and Bob Lillquist, her sister, Ellen, and brother, Robbie, on Christmas. We had a leg of lamb for dinner and the adults (except for Mike) enjoyed wine with the meal.

Pat and I hit it off immediately. We discussed why each of us wouldn't have liked the other's kid just a couple of years earlier.

Janet was rebellious.

Mike was a drunk.

They both were pathologically stubborn.

But whose kid was worse? It didn't matter, although she hadn't had to impose a rule about discussing felonies with Mommy.

Mike fit into the family really well, and after dinner, Bob showed us some of his military memorabilia, including some World War II helmets, both American and German.

The helmets were out for just a few minutes before Bob and Mike had donned them and were singing "Springtime for Hitler." Bob was waving a glass of wine as he sang—Mike a bottle of Coke.

"Join us, Mom," Mike insisted.

"Oh, I can't. I only see two helmets."

Bob had more.

He also had medical instrument kits from the Civil War, antique rifles, and more. The house was practically a military museum, and Mike was fascinated by all the history.

Mike went to work for a fine-dining restaurant, then a chain restaurant where he might be able to get health insurance (it turned out to be very expensive and covered little more than the insurance company's ass), and then as a manager for an Auntie Anne's Pretzel store in the mall. He hated malls even before he went to work for Auntie Anne's, but he hoped he could rise in the organization and get group health insurance, since he wouldn't be able to get it on his own.

It didn't work out that way, and he became increasingly frustrated at the unfulfilled promises of his bosses and the unreliability of the teenagers who worked for him.

The kicker came around Thanksgiving. On Black Friday, a family of animatronic bears appeared outside Auntie Anne's. They sang "We Wish You a Merry Christmas" in one endless, hellish loop.

"I wanna take a fuckin' baseball bat to them," he said again and again. "I just wanna beat them to a quivering fuckin' pulp."

When no one was looking, Mike unplugged the display, but someone always plugged it back in.

The shoppers were no more pleasing than the bears. Mike had a very low threshold for rudeness, but he had to be nice to customers even as they cursed him out for not being fast enough or not having what they wanted.

The experience ruined Christmas for him.

"I'm sure the baby Jesus would be at the mall dancing with the fuckin' bears, but I've had enough of it," he said.

Mike always loved Thanksgiving because it focused on family, on gratitude, and on food. If he was at my house for dinner, we had to double the amount of dressing and gravy we made because he ate as much as the rest of us put together, then he would eat a couple pieces of chocolate cream pie. He and Danny both loved the turkey potpie I made with the leftovers, which meant I had to make at least two pies if Rob and I wanted any.

Thanksgiving also included listening to Arlo Guthrie's "Alice's Restaurant," which WNEW-FM in New York played every Thanksgiving morning. After dinner, we watched the original *King Kong*, which WPIX TV ran every Thanksgiving afternoon. We knew all the lyrics to "Alice's Restaurant," and we knew all the dialogue to *King Kong*, so we sang and spoke along.

To Mike, Thanksgiving meant family, food and fun, which were so much better than the greed and consumerism surrounding Christmas—although he didn't mind getting presents.

Chapter 13

In 1999, Mike and Janet announced their engagement. They would marry on June 2, 2000. Instead of leaving all the planning to Janet, Mike decided he would be in charge of the food and the music.

Mike was picky about both. In fact, Danny hated to go to restaurants with Mike because he picked the place apart like a *New York Times* food critic. The waiter might put the plate down on the wrong side or not recall who ordered which dish. The meat or vegetables might be slightly overcooked, the coffee weak, the salad wilted . . .

"I don't think he ever enjoys it," Danny told me.

"Sure he enjoys it," I said. "He also enjoys criticizing it."

I've seen him call the waiter over and politely ask, "Is this the chef's idea of rare?"

He could be critical, but I never saw him be rude to wait staff, nor was he ever rude to a customer, even when someone complained that the red wine wasn't cold or ordered a fine steak well done. He preferred to work in restaurants where the chef refused to cook a steak more than medium. That way, he didn't have to be responsible for serving "ruined" beef.

Danny had lived in South Georgia long enough to become a true Southerner. He had acquired the accent. He tried to deny it, but New Yorkers don't say, "fixin' tuh," when they're getting ready to do something. His accent became firmly Southern when he joined the US Marine Reserves in 1993. The only vestige of his Northeast upbringing was his enduring love of the New York Yankees. When Peyton was born in February of 1993, one of the first things he did was buy her an infant-sized Yankees uniform and take her around to visit all of his friends who were Braves fans.

Mike, on the other hand, was "New Yawk" to the core. He had a thick New York accent, he was loud and bawdy, often profane, and he had a very twisted sense of humor. Janet was perfect for him because she shared his sense of the absurd.

Janet didn't know much about southern cooking. When visiting Danny and Jennifer in Brunswick, she went to a restaurant and tried to order chicken fried steak rare. When she was informed it only came well done, she ordered something else and suffered Danny's and Mike's teasing through the rest of the meal.

"How was I to know it's breaded and fried like chicken?" she asked. "That's an awful thing to do to beef."

Mike wanted a live band for the wedding because, as a musician, he preferred live music. He auditioned a number of bands before settling on one, which ended up pulling out a few weeks before the wedding and sent him into a panic.

They found an old Victorian mansion with a gorgeous garden for the ceremony and reception and a photographer who would take photos in both color and black and white. The only thing I asked for was a portrait of me and Rob, both boys, the grandmothers, daughters-in-law, and grandchildren. I never got it. We were all there, ready to sit for the picture when we discovered the photographer had left already.

The granddaughters were to be the flower girls. After weeks of shopping for appropriate dresses, we gave up and Janet's mother offered to sew long skirts for them. Everything we looked at was far too grown up for girls aged four, seven, and eight, even though it was made in their sizes. We found plunging necklines and tight bodices, but nothing we were comfortable dressing our little girls in.

As I was stitching madly to finish a hand-pieced, hand-quilted, queen-sized quilt for them, Mike and Janet asked me to crochet a cover for a satin pillow for the ring bearer (Janet's brother, Robbie). I had no excuse to refuse unless I spoiled the surprise of the quilt, so I agreed. I finished both just days before the wedding.

The week before the wedding, Danny and Jennifer came up from Georgia and spent a couple of days with us. Our new grandson, Trey, was just three months old.

Danny was best man and he was agonizing over the toast.

"I don't speak in public," he said. "What am I supposed to say?"

He wasn't comfortable with anything anyone suggested. Frankly, I wouldn't have been comfortable with much of what was suggested.

Once we got to the hotel in Albany, together with the rest of the family and most of our New Jersey friends, the party began in earnest. We were celebrating more than just a wedding; we were celebrating Michael's rebirth and our confidence that he had a great future.

The afternoon we got there, I called Mike and asked him to meet us at Janet's mother's house when he got off work.

"I hate it when people make plans for me without consulting me," he said.

"I have your wedding present," I said.

"Oh. OK."

Neither of them suspected I had made a quilt for them, and when they saw it, they unfurled it and wrapped it around themselves.

"Mommy made me a new blankie!" he said. I didn't know it, but he still had his old "boo bankie."

Both sets of parents and stepparents were at the rehearsal and at the dinner. Danny was nervous, as always, that we might not all be civil, but we got along fine. One of my favorite pictures from the rehearsal was of "the four dads," talking together on the back porch of the mansion.

On the morning of the wedding, several of us women went to brunch with Janet. A few minutes after we sat down, Danny called Jennifer to tell her he had lost Mike's wedding ring. Jennifer stayed calm, knowing it was probably in the pocket of his tux, but he kept calling, panicked because he knew this was going to ruin the wedding.

"I put it where I was sure I wouldn't forget it and I forgot where I put it!" he said. "It's gone. It's just gone!"

Knowing that Danny is prone to panic, much the way his father was, we finished brunch. By the time we got back, the motel room was torn apart. Within a few minutes, Jennifer had it pretty much back together and had found the ring.

Danny still hadn't settled on a toast.

"I think I'm just going to say, 'Over the lips and past the gums; look out liver here it comes,'" he said.

"At least wish them happiness," I pleaded.

He did, just before he said, "Over the lips . . ." Fortunately, Mike and Janet were amused and not offended.

As the time of the ceremony drew near, a line of severe thunderstorms came through, and Janet was trapped at the hairdresser for forty minutes. Mike wandered the Victorian mansion asking whether anyone had heard from Janet and when he might expect her to arrive. It was still raining when she arrived thirty minutes late and still had to get dressed. Everything was so drenched that performing the ceremony outside was impossible.

Janet wore a white tea-length dress with crimson silk under the lace above the waist and ruby-red shoes. She wore red roses woven into her hair and carried a dozen long-stemmed red roses.

My mother described her as "sassy and lovely."

Although Mike and many of the guests didn't drink, the bar was open for those of us who wanted wine or beer. It was hard to tell who was drinking (guests could choose either champagne or sparkling cider for the toast) because everyone was encouraged to act silly. Every place setting had a jar of bubble solution and every table had a camera.

We were able to do one old folks' tradition—Rob's friend, John Wiley, led a "soul train." John, who dances much as Mike and I, led a conga line of sorts with about seventy-five of the one hundred guests. The room was barely big enough for the line, and some chairs did get knocked over. The soul train is something John has led at more than a dozen weddings now, but Mike's was the first of the kids' weddings.

During the reception, several of Mike's friends from his twelve-step group came over to tell me how much he had helped them along their road to sobriety. "He saved my life," a couple of them said. Lest I think they were just using the expression lightly, one of them made certain I knew it was "literally, man, literally."

Mike's old high school friend, Andrew Koval, came, and I think Mike and Andrew danced as much as Mike and Janet.

Mike was not a graceful dancer, but he loved to get out on the dance floor and move. When it came time for the groom-mother dance, Mike grabbed me and tangoed me across the floor, dipping me at the end of each sweep. It was fine because I'm not much of a dancer, either, and it was exactly what everyone expected.

After the wedding reception, the party was in Rob's and my hotel room. It wasn't wild, but it was funny. Rob's friend, Craig McKeown, known among his friends and family as the world's most obnoxious man, told Southern jokes that had Danny doubled over.

"I should be so offended," Danny said several times. But he just kept laughing. Weeks later, Danny called me and repeated that he couldn't understand why he didn't get mad at Craig, but he still laughed whenever he thought of the remarks.

The kids weren't planning on a honeymoon because their finances were tight, so family members and friends got together and wrote checks for them to travel to Toronto and have at least one fabulous dinner—even by their standards.

Not long after the wedding, Mike took a job managing a Stewart's convenience store. The job would offer some basic health insurance, so he could get a colonoscopy, but he hated the job.

Mike's colonoscopy showed some scar tissue around where the ureters were implanted into the sigmoid colon, but there was no cancer—yet. Because his father had been diagnosed with colon cancer, Mike's chances of getting it increased to one in four.

Hazen was diagnosed with stage 3 colorectal cancer just after the wedding. The chemo was grueling and had to be stopped early because of its extreme effects on him. The radiation damaged nerves in his spine, leaving him unable to walk without assistance—braces and a walker.

"I'm so disillusioned," Mike told me. "I thought Dad was a perfect asshole."

That was Mike's way of dealing with horror—he cracked inappropriate jokes. But he knew he was likely to suffer the same fate.

Because of his excellent insurance, Hazen could obtain care anywhere he wanted; he chose the Mayo Clinic, which had a clinic in Jacksonville, Florida, an hour south of Brunswick. He would travel to Minnesota for some of his care, but his chemotherapy and radiation would be administered in Jacksonville.

Six months after his diagnosis, I ran into him and Linda at Trey's first birthday party. He looked pale and sickly; Linda looked exhausted.

"How are you doing, Linda?" I asked.

Her eyes began to tear up. She talked about her fears and how it tore her apart to see Hazen suffer from the ravaging effects of chemo and radiation. We talked for about an hour.

Later that night, Danny joked about how my new best friend and I had such a great time. I lit into him.

"How could you go six months and never once ask Linda how she's handling all this?" I demanded.

"Well, it's Dad who's sick," he said.

Yes, Hazen was facing possible death, but Linda was facing something just as frightening—a future without him. She was the one driving him to and from chemo and radiation. She was the one who had to care for him when he was too sick or weak to do things for himself.

"You live right here in the same town," I said. "Maybe you should stop over there now and then and see if there's anything you can do for them."

Danny took the advice to heart, and afterward he made sure Linda's needs were considered too.

Twice more, Hazen's doctors would find small cancerous growths and remove them, but he survived the cancer. He was forced to retire early, and he had no trouble getting Social Security Disability, so he never had to be without an income. He still had health insurance, and two years after getting Disability, he became eligible for Medicare. He never had to worry about his medical expenses.

It was a hard year for Hazen and Linda and for their son, Scott, and for my boys. Cancer is a frightening diagnosis. Just the word makes my heart sink. I offered a lot of encouragement that year.

Since Hazen never was good at being still, his retirement was difficult at first, especially since he couldn't play golf, which had been his favorite pastime his whole life. He saw almost every movie that came out; he went out to lunch almost every day; he went to the dog track . . . he slowly learned how to fill his time.

Chapter 14

In September 2001, I was in my office at the nursing journal, *RN*, waiting for an announcement on layoffs when Rob sent me an e-mail from his office in lower Manhattan. The World Trade Center was on fire, but he was fine.

I turned on the radio to hear that an airplane had hit one of the Twin Towers. As I listened, the other tower was hit. This wasn't some freak accident; we were under attack, and Rob was just twelve blocks away, watching events unfold through the window of his office.

As the second building fell, debris billowed through the streets; the cloud stopped just a block away from Rob's building.

Soon afterward, we heard that the Pentagon had been hit and another plane had been forced down in a field in Pennsylvania.

Everyone in the office knew people who worked in the Twin Towers. One woman's son worked on one of the highest floors and she was certain he was dead, but she didn't want to go home and be alone. Another woman had a relative who worked in the Pentagon.

We all waited to hear more, but word was slow in coming because phone service was out in Lower Manhattan; even cell phones weren't working.

Finally, at about one o'clock, word came that the first woman's son had overslept and was down in the subway station when the first plane hit; the other woman's relative in the Pentagon also was safe.

Late in the afternoon, Mike finally got through to me. He knew I had a job interview in Manhattan sometime that week. It was scheduled for Friday and it was near Times Square, but all Mike could think was that it had been that day—September 11—and that it was at the World Trade Center.

He and Danny were in a panic. How close had Rob been? Was he OK too? They couldn't reach him.

Rob left the office at about noon and walked six miles north to Grand Central Station, where he caught a train uptown and then a bus out of the city. It was after six when he finally called to say the bus had dropped him in Tarrytown, across the Hudson River from us.

I had called around to a number of friends who should have been in the building, but not one of them was there when the planes hit. One had taken the day off; another had gone out to pick up coffee and doughnuts for a meeting; another was sick that day. In all, we only knew one person who died in the attack.

The kids in my Sunday school class knew several of the casualties, though. They wanted to know why God would allow such a thing to happen.

"God gave humans free will," I said. "This is what some choose to do with it."

Coverage was nonstop for days, but Rob couldn't bear to watch it. Seeing it happen live was enough to last him a lifetime.

The following week, Shannon was getting married in Massachusetts and the entire family would meet there. Mike saw Rob from across the motel parking lot and raced over to embrace him.

"I was scared shitless," he said. "I just want you to know I love you and I'm so glad nothing happened to you."

He turned toward me. "Oh, hi, Mom," he said.

Dan Dore, the minister who was supposed to marry Matt and Shannon had gone to Manhattan as a first responder. The minister who stood in for him used the "love, honor and obey" vow, and I imagined Shannon crossing her fingers as she recited the word "obey." The rest of the Boyd women and Mike all suppressed a chuckle. We Boyd women don't blindly obey anyone; we think for ourselves and we take pride in our strength. Pastor Dan would have known that, and when he heard about it later, he got a good laugh out of it.

Shannon was a beautiful bride, and her brother, Stephen, looked incredibly handsome in his dress Army uniform as he walked her down the aisle.

I lost my job at the nursing journal a week after 9/11. I knew it was coming and I already had a few irons in the fire. I was confident I could find another job pretty quickly, so I decided to enjoy my time off.

But three weeks later, Rob learned that he would lose his job December 1. The economy was tanking as a result of the attacks.

I had a meeting at the church that night with Bonnie Harmon, who always tends to look on the bright side of things.

"Oh, how exciting," she said. "Where do you think your next adventure will be?"

Adventure? Rob and I were both about to be unemployed in one of the most expensive parts of the country. Disaster was a better word for what was happening.

Bonnie shook her head. "Just trust," she said. "Go home and listen for that still, small voice. God always has a plan if you care to find out what it is. Listen, and you'll probably think it's your own idea."

Bonnie always believed—a little more strongly than I did—that God intervenes in our daily lives.

"Just be calm and wait," she said as we parted.

That night as I was trying to fall asleep, a thought came to me.

Richard Leonard, who had hired me at two different newspapers, had moved into Gannett Corporate as recruiter for the entire News Division. I could call him.

The next morning I made the call. I told him how the attacks had made me realize how much I missed the newspaper business; that was true. I wanted to be the one telling others what was going on, not the one waiting to hear. I missed being able to change government policy with a good investigative article.

I was an experienced reporter with a good reputation and Rob was a crack copyeditor with a fabulous reputation. Richard was sure he could find us something. Where did we want to go?

Anywhere in the Northeast—or Asheville, North Carolina, I said.

"Why Asheville?" he asked.

"Obviously you haven't been there," I answered. "It's a beautiful place and the culture and music are wonderful."

"I'll get back to you in a few days," he said.

Rob and I decided to take a long weekend and go camping in Vermont. As we sat by the campfire, I told him I was certain we'd have a message from Richard when we got home that there were two jobs in either Burlington, Vermont, or Asheville.

"You're spending too much time alone," Rob said. "In the real world you're not a size three; it does rain during the daytime and jobs don't just happen like that."

But I was right. Richard had called and left a message that there were two jobs in Asheville.

We talked to the executive editor, Bob Gabordi, over the phone. He seemed like the type of boss I wanted and we were a good fit with what he was looking for. He sent us some newspapers to critique.

In early November, we flew into Asheville for the interview. I really liked Bob and the reporters and editors I met. On Thursday night, Bob offered us the jobs and we accepted. We would start on January 2, 2002.

Danny and Jennifer and the kids were happy to have us five hours away instead of sixteen. We were just an hour from the cabins where we had vacationed with them.

Two weeks later, we were back to look for a house. Our house in New York went under contract for the full asking price its first day on the market. We went to Asheville armed with a list of places we wanted to see and a real estate agent to guide us. We found what we wanted—a three-bedroom house on a full acre of land.

The next day we visited a Congregational church, which we have attended ever since. The pastor's sermon talked about the disastrous environmental policies of the Bush administration and its refusal to acknowledge global warming. Then a committee chair stood up to talk about gay and lesbian issues.

Now, I refuse to attend a church that would not have welcomed my sister and her spouse, so it was good to have the question of gay rights answered for me. But this church was taking it a little further—it was about to vote on becoming an "open and affirming" church, the United Church of Christ denomination's language for a church that stands up for LGBT rights.

Rob and I were ready to join before the service was over, and a few weeks after we moved to Asheville, we did just that.

Everything fell into place so easily it seemed as though this move was meant to be.

Soon after I started working at the paper, Bob Gabordi called me into his office. As the father of a daughter with profound disabilities, Bob was concerned about the policies in North Carolina. He knew a lot of families were waiting for care they deserved through the state's Medicaid Waiver program, CAP MR-DD—Community Access Program for children with Mental Retardation and Developmental Disabilities, and he wanted to know if I was interested in doing an investigative piece on the issue.

I hadn't had time to develop a lot of sources, but I did have Annie Doucette, an old friend of my sister, Ellen. They had worked together at Wrentham State School and now Annie was in charge of the Developmental Disabilities program at Blue Ridge Area Program, the regional agency that managed the care of people with DD, mental illness, and addiction. She described the program for me. In essence, it provides money for families with children with DD so they can care for their children at home rather than in an institution.

No one knew how many people were eligible for CAP MR-DD because no one was declared eligible until he or she actually got into the program. However, no one had gotten in for five years.

So, how many people were waiting? No one knew. And why was the program frozen for five years? No one knew. Was there a way to get more people into the program? No one knew.

I found a family to follow: Dana and Mike Hartis and Dana's ten-year-old son, Ethan Gray, who had autism and Down syndrome. As it was, Mike and Dana were paying $3,000 every time Ethan's teeth were cleaned because he had to be anesthetized. They wanted an adaptive bicycle for him, but it was more than they could afford.

When Ethan had a tantrum in the middle of a store or in a street or parking lot, he had to be physically picked up and moved to safety, but he weighed 100 pounds—almost as much as Dana, and she was pregnant.

I spent time with the family every week, and when little Maggie was born, I was their third phone call. Dana and I are still friends, although she and Mike are divorced.

Dana and I laughed at how Ethan tried to move Maggie's crib out of the house. Maggie's crying set Ethan off into a meltdown, and he decided it was time for her to move out. The dog could stay, but the sister had to go. He never tried to harm Maggie, but it was clear how he felt.

I went to Raleigh to interview people in government and in advocacy organizations. I called national sources and interviewed people from other states about their programs and how they managed to fund them. I read a ton of reports and studies about the effectiveness of Medicaid Waiver programs and how other states handled them. I sent questionnaires out to every Area Program in North Carolina inquiring as to how many people were waiting for five of a list of ten services covered by CAP; they all got back to me.

It turned out almost two thousand families would qualify for CAP MR-DD if it were made available to them; there were about two thousand families being served already.

The way CAP was funded—each person got a "slot" with funding for up to $87,000. If a person only used $20,000 of the allotment, the balance of the money couldn't go to fund someone else. The program was based on slots, not funding, which saved the state a lot of money, but cost families a lot more in money, stress, and anxiety.

Ten months after I started work, the piece was ready to go. I had written it all in one take and would break it up into a dozen or more stories.

I was afraid Bob wouldn't like the piece, although I don't know why, but he declared it "incredible."

Three days before publication, someone from the state Department of Health and Human Services called to say the state was changing the way CAP MR-DD was funded. Instead of the slot approach, each family would receive what it needed, up to $87,000, and any money not used would go back into CAP to fund more people.

The following Sunday, "Ethan's Story," a twelve-page special section was published. It would win state and national awards, but the best part was that five months later, Ethan got into CAP MR-DD.

We had changed state policy with my investigation and it was the best feeling I ever had as a reporter. It had happened before and it would happen several times more, but this was the best.

Chapter 15

Mike and Janet both were working for Stewart's, a convenience store chain, in 2002. Mike was managing a store and was becoming increasingly frustrated with the job—its low pay and horrendous work hours and its unreliable employees. He began to worry whether he could stay at the company and maintain his sobriety.

Since his most recent colonoscopy showed there was some scar tissue around the implant site and a couple of noncancerous polyps, he decided to take a chance. Before he had insurance, he had been able to get a colonoscopy every year in New York and pay it off in installments. He figured that if he went back to college, he could keep doing that. He gambled that he would stay healthy for four years.

Janet wanted to finish a four-year degree, too, so she began applying to art schools. Mike figured he would find a college wherever Janet was accepted.

That turned out to be the Savannah College of Art and Design in Georgia, just an hour from Danny. Mike applied and got accepted into Armstrong Atlantic University, a Georgia state school. He decided he would major in history and minor in philosophy.

"That's just great," I said. "I mean, the wants ads are full of employers looking for historians and philosophers."

"This isn't my last stop," he told me. "I'm going on to law school. I want to help people who can't afford a good lawyer, and I'm going to be a good lawyer."

Once it was settled that they would move to Savannah, Mike took a few days off to drive down and look for a place for them to live. He stopped to spend a couple of days with us. Because our friends, Craig and Cindy McKeown, also were visiting, he offered to stay in the backyard in his tent, since he was planning to camp out in Savannah to save the cost of a hotel room.

Of course, the joke all weekend was about Mike living in a tent in our backyard again, but it was easy to laugh now because Mike had come so far. Instead of being a drunk, Mike was chasing drunks. Instead of being angry, he was funny and content with the direction his life was taking. He was eager to get back to school.

Once again, he laughed easily and often. Working in restaurants, he had gained an appreciation of good food, although he was still known to heat up a frozen pizza and devour the whole thing.

"Salt and grease. My two favorite food groups," he said.

As goofy as he acted much of the time, there was a maturity about him now. Danielle described it as the wisdom of a person who had been to the precipice and back. Most people hit bottom before they get to the very edge; a few fall into the abyss, and a very few make it to the very edge before they wave their arms in backward windmills and stagger back. That was Mike, and the experience had given him a deep appreciation for everything in life.

Having him back made me love him even more fiercely. His soul was the mirror to mine. I knew what he was thinking before he ever spoke it, especially if it was a wisecrack.

He claimed his darker self still lived inside of him, but it was under control. It was like that Star Trek episode with the two Captain Kirks . . . not the parallel universe evil Kirk, but the one split in two by the transporter. Its moral was that we all need our darker side.

Mike and I related a lot of things to Star Trek episodes. It made us laugh. We had a few friends who were as geeky as we were about it, and who could have lengthy pseudo-debates about how real life was reflected in Star Trek episodes. We spoke snippets of dialogue and we all knew which episode the lines came from.

Yeah, it was odd, but so were we, and we took pride in it. He had gained wisdom through his ride to hell and back, and his humor sometimes had an uncomfortable edge.

Once, when I asked him what was going in inside his head, he replied, "Oh, you don't want to be in here. I'm not even comfortable in here." It was a joke, but it had a mildly disturbing morsel of truth.

A few days after he left our house, Mike rented a mobile home in a gated park. A two-bedroom mobile home with a big kitchen was far cheaper than an apartment with the same amount of space, and he would have room for a small garden. The soil and the climate were perfect for hot peppers.

The landlord accepted pets, so Finley and Pandora would make the trip—sedated. Mike and Janet wouldn't have rented a place where they couldn't bring the cats, but they knew better than to try and bring them without sedation.

Mike and Janet packed everything they had into a big U-Haul and hooked the car to a tow-bar. They drove I-81 through New York, Pennsylvania, and Virginia. Instead of going forty or so miles out of their way into Tennessee, they decided to take a secondary road to hook up with I-26 in North Carolina.

But in the mountains of Tennessee and North Carolina, secondary highways often climb and descend the landscape in steep, harrowing S-curves and switchbacks. They hit the worst of it as the cats' sedation wore off.

"It looked fine on the fuckin' map," Mike said when he got to the house, exhausted and frazzled. The cats were yowling, as they had been for more than an hour. "From here on, I stay on the fuckin' interstate, even if I have to go a hundred fuckin' mikes out of my fuckin' way."

He put on a pot of coffee and settled in to sulk on the couch for awhile before supper. We closed off the family room downstairs and released Finley and Pandora, who didn't seem a whole lot happier being free in an unfamiliar place—and they would not have been happy to meet Beasley, our sixty-pound Labrador retriever mix.

It was good to know Mike and Janet would be closer now. I would be able to see them on my way to visit Danny and Jennifer and the kids, and Savannah was a city I wanted to see. Its history and architecture are fascinating and I was looking forward to exploring it with Mike and Janet, along with the coastal area between there and Brunswick.

Mike and I had been to Catalouchee Valley a couple of times with our cameras and we both wanted to get some good pictures of the marshes, lighthouses, and fishing boats along the Georgia coast.

It didn't take long for Mike and Janet to find some great restaurants in Savannah. We never went to Paula Deen's Lady & Sons because it was too crowded and Mike insisted there was food elsewhere that was just as good or better—and less expensive.

So we went to a Moroccan restaurant where we ate with our fingers and a Vietnamese/Asian fusion restaurant. We sampled Indian and Italian, and of course, Low Country cuisine.

Along the waterfront we found a fun toy store and great ice cream. He knew the best coffee shops within a week of moving to Savannah, helped, he said, by his new twelve-step friends.

Finding a twelve-step group was the first thing Mike did whenever he arrived in a new place, even places he was just visiting. It gave him a center. If he visited a place more than twice, he always had a twelve-step group he could go to.

I visited fairly frequently, and I slept on a futon in the spare bedroom, often with one or another of the cats. Before long, there was Jerry. He was a cat who demanded attention and adoration, an in-your-face creature with a motorboat purr. The next-door neighbors had moved out and left him behind.

Soon after they took in Jerry, several kittens appeared. Mike and Janet left food out on the deck for them. One of the kittens, a tabby male, had a hip deformity. We called him Ack, (for Awfully Cute Kitty, or Ass Crud Kitty, depending on whom you asked), although he never was allowed in the house because he was unable to clean his hindquarters. Of all the kittens, he was the most friendly and affectionate.

"Don't go near his ass," Mike told me every time I went to pet Ack. "It needs to be cleaned."

He didn't like being cleaned, but he sometimes would allow it.

There was plenty of wildlife around the house. A possum came by regularly to nibble on the cat food and would saunter away if caught by humans. It apparently knew no one was going to harm it, at least not at that house.

A black snake lived in the creek (actually a ditch with water) at the back of the property, and we sat and took photos as it caught and ate a frog. We also captured a few photos of a toad eating a moth on the deck late one night.

Mike was a sucker for animals. One night as he was driving home from work waiting tables at Tony Roma's, he saw a car hit a dog and keep driving. Mike stopped and scooped the dog up into his arms, wrapped it in a blanket he had in the backseat, and brought it home, hoping to find a vet who could see it at that late hour.

He sat, dialing the phone as he stroked the badly injured dog. He held it tenderly as it died. It seemed to be a stray, he told me later, after he had buried it under the pine tree in his backyard and sobbed for awhile. He so desperately wanted to find help for the animal, but it was late at night and he wasn't able to find an emergency vet.

"No one deserves to be abandoned like that, not even a dog," he said. He had a few thoughts about what the driver of the car—and the person who allowed the dog to roam free—deserved.

"At least he had the comfort of being loved at the end of his life," Mike said. "Every creature deserves at least that much."

Mike loved being able to have a garden—mostly hot peppers and some herbs, which he couldn't grow in Schenectady because the growing season was too short. We all shared in the abundance of peppers that year, and Mike took almost daily photos to document the progress of his crop. He planted some morning glories, his favorite flower, and watched all through the summer as the vines climbed up the oak tree in the front and along the railings of the deck.

Mike and Janet both found jobs at a restaurant and pub called Tony Roma's. Mike waited tables—he'd had enough of cooking—and Janet tended bar.

Not long after they settled in, Jennifer called to tell me that Danny had been badly burned at work. A valve had failed and sprayed him with scalding hot caustic chemicals. He had second- and third-degree burns over about 40 percent of his body, mostly his legs.

I drove down to Georgia that morning. Danny had already been sent home because there are for more dangerous germs in the hospital than at anyone's house.

"OK," I said when I got there. "First of all, no one touches you without first washing their hands with antibacterial soap. Second, you need to be drinking water constantly so you don't get dehydrated."

"Oh, like you know all about burns," he said.

Having written about health issues for 25 years, two of them at a nursing journal, I did know a bit about treating burns, among other things.

A nurse would visit once or twice every day, and when she arrived for her first visit, she told everyone—pretty much verbatim—what I had said.

I had to learn to change his bandages because Jennifer fainted at the sight of the burns. I didn't have a problem with it. I stayed for a little over a week until Danny was feeling better. With pain medication, he was able to cope pretty well. But the pain medication would leave worse scars than the burns.

He would battle his dependence on them for years.

Michael, age five months, after his bath.

Michael, age 6, at the office of the weekly newspaper, The Rockland Review. Photo by Kathy Gardner.

Michael and his grandfather, age 8 months

Michael, age 3, at his grandfather's house in Massachusetts.

Michael and Danny at Rob's and my wedding reception.

Michael and Danny at Rob's and my wedding reception. Michael nearly always hammed it up for the camera. He usually was serious only when threatened.

High school graduation day. He was delivered to his graduation on a classic red and white Indian motorcycle restored by our next door neighbor and his mentor, Charlie Frey.

Michael, age 15, at Plymouth, Massachusetts. This was three months after his grandfather's death, during what became known as the Crazy Whale Watch Weekend.

Mike and Danny with Meghan, at their Grandma Elise's funeral in 1997.

Mike and Janet soon after they began dating.

Mike and Janet at Krispy Kreme.

At Mike and Janet's wedding. Danny made Mike pose "like a human being – a grownup human being."

The infamous gigantic Christmas tree.

Two seconds after the first photo was shot, Mike had a silly face.

Mike and Ellen (right) with Ellen's spouse, KJ, just after playing the Cancer Card to get to the head of the food line at our annual family picnic in July 2007. Ellen would die three weeks later.

The groom and mother dance at Mike's wedding

Mike at a miniature golf course on Jekyll Island, Georgia. The gorilla is still there.

Chapter 16

Between studies and work, Mike and Janet didn't have a lot of time for gardening or other hobbies.

Mike's and Janet's jobs paid the bills, but they didn't provide health insurance. Fortunately, both of them could get care for simple ailments on campus.

Mike had thought he would be able to be billed for his annual colonoscopies, but the gastroenterology practice in Savannah refused to do the procedure unless Mike paid them $2,300 up front. No insurance, no credit. Cash only.

It didn't matter that Mike was a student with a low-paying job; in fact, it probably cemented their resolve not to help him by refusing to let him pay it off at $200 a month. Medicine is a business and businesses don't like to take credit risks.

Mike didn't tell his family about this because he didn't want us to worry. He just took it a day at a time.

I did get to see Mike and Janet more often, as my trips to Georgia were more likely to be three- or four-day weekends, and Mike and Janet came to Asheville for holidays.

One of their first trips here was Thanksgiving. Rob was working, so we planned the family meal for the next day. I took them on what I call the Waterfall Tour, meandering out of Asheville, southwest through Brevard and then Jackson County, west across US Route 64 and then down US 441 to Dillard, Georgia, and the Dillard House, a restaurant that offers southern cooking served up family style.

We had stopped at a couple of places—Looking Glass Falls and DuPont State Park—before we got to Whitewater Falls, the highest waterfall in the United States east of the Rocky Mountains.

"So, can you see why I love it here?" I asked as we stood looking at the waterfall.

He leaned on the fence and looked at me, smiling. "Mom, I've never seen you this happy."

He was right. I had grown up in a small town; my formative years were spent on a farm, and I had lived in the suburbs of New York City for as long as Mike could remember—he was two and a half when we moved from Georgia. I never liked living in crowded conditions and I never felt quite at home in New York. It was difficult to find supplies for quilting or crocheting or home canning and most people seemed more concerned with being in a rush than with enjoying their lives.

The mountain culture is slower, more friendly, and a whole lot cheaper. We grow more of our own food here and we know the farmers who produce much of what we buy. Much of the art comes from the old culture, when the remote nature of the mountains led to people making their own pottery and furniture, their own clothing and quilts. These utilitarian things began being embellished, and people come here now just to buy them and to hear the music and the storytellers.

We continued on, stopping at Dry Falls and Bridal Veil Falls, and finally ending up at the Dillard House.

If you've never been there, they explain the drill: For one price, they bring out all that they've cooked that day, and you eat. If you finish one dish and want more of it, they'll bring it. Often, when a waiter comes by and people's mouths are full, a point with a fork and a mumbled "thank you" are all that's needed.

We ate turkey and country ham, cabbage and cheese casserole, potatoes, cornbread, cranberry sauce, green beans, fried chicken, and more. Dessert was peach cobbler and Janet had three helpings. We ate for an hour before we finally sat back to enjoy a cup of coffee.

Janet sat back and looked toward the window.

"Oh look!" she gasped. "There's a view!"

For New Year's Eve that first year, everyone came—Danny and Jennifer, the four grandkids, and Mike and Janet—ten people in our little house. No one objected to the crowding, least of all Beasley, who had all the attention any dog could want. If one person grew weary of throwing a tennis ball in the backyard, someone else would step in.

Until that time, Trey had been afraid of dogs, but he warmed up to Beasley that visit—helped by Mike rolling on the floor with the dog. For the rest of the visit, Trey and Beasley were inseparable.

When the dog kissed Trey on his face, we all reminded him that Beasley licks his butt and eats cat poop if he can get to it.

"I don't care," Trey said to everyone's disgust. "I love him."

It felt good to have the whole family together, even though it was just for a couple of days. My boys finally got along, although that meant they ganged up on me.

Danny had a good job and Michael was headed in the right direction, doing well at school and maintaining his sobriety.

My job was going well—I already had managed to change state policy once with "Ethan's Story," and the state was gearing up for big changes in its mental health system.

Of course, I was writing stories about people who needed health care but didn't have access. I wrote about fund-raisers to help pay for chemotherapy and doctors' bills. I wrote about a program called Project Access that helped uninsured and underinsured people gain access to the specialty care they needed.

But Project Access, like many other programs, relied on doctors and hospitals donating care; it did nothing to address the systemic problems that kept people from getting care.

I wrote about a charity run by a local women's cancer practice because the doctors couldn't, in good conscience, allow women who needed chemotherapy to forego it because they couldn't afford it.

I had been writing about the health insurance crisis since 1992, when sixteen million people were uninsured. One little girl wrote to then President-elect Bill Clinton to ask him to do something about it. He wrote her back, promising to try.

As I wrote these stories I didn't know Mike wasn't getting the care he needed. I didn't know Savannah had nothing like Project Access. I knew the emergency room wasn't the answer because I knew the ER only has to stabilize patients, not look for the cause. I didn't know what a problem this would cause for my son and my family.

In Raleigh, meanwhile, the state was gearing up to overhaul the mental health, developmental disability, and substance abuse services programs.

Before "reform," people could go to a local agency, called an area program, for assessment, services, and case management. Reform closed the area programs, privatized the services, and opened "local management entities," or LMEs, to manage the privatized network of services.

Several of the area programs spun their services off into nonprofit treatment centers, hoping no one who needed services would be lost in the shuffle.

It all looked great on paper. People would have a choice about where to get their services, and a "robust" network of community services would grow and thrive because of competition.

But weeks before the transition, the state still had not finalized the Medicaid definitions—essentially a job description of services that would be paid for—and they had not published rates.

I asked someone at the state Department of Health and Human Services whether anyone was signing up to provide services, and the person admitted there was no stampede in the private sector to sign on.

"Well, if I'm applying for a job, but you can't give me a job description or tell me what I'll be paid, do you think I should pursue that job?" I asked.

She waved a dismissive hand in my direction. "Oh, they know the rates are Medicaid rates."

While state government officials talked about "consumer choice" and "flexibility to offer a wider array of services," service providers were worried whether they would be able to stay afloat with Medicaid rates, and whether they could provide the services that would be required.

The system as it existed wasn't perfect, but it was doing OK. It was rated twenty-third in the country, so there was room for improvement, but most people who had been in mental health services for a long time worried about what this new system would bring.

One of the most experienced administrators in the state told me he saw it as a train wreck. I wasn't sure what to think of his assessment because when I met him, he was onstage answering questions about the new system—which was just months from being implemented—and all he could say was, "We don't know that yet," or, "That hasn't been figured out yet."

I thought this was either the most inept man alive or the state was in a heap of trouble.

Turns out the administrator was right; it became a train wreck. Within a couple of years, North Carolina's mental health system would fall within the bottom five in the nation. Because it wasn't well planned before it was launched, it needed serious overhaul from the beginning.

Within months, the nonprofits were failing, and the secretary of DHHS was changing the rules almost weekly.

"Reform" would keep me busy for several years.

I also wrote frequently about people caught in the health care system, bankrupted, and still needing care. If they were lucky enough to get onto the front page of one of the paper's sections, they would get money pouring in.

It seemed every time I wrote about one case, I received a dozen calls, begging me to publicize another person who would die without treatment.

I went on writing about problems in the health and mental health care systems, hoping Mike and Janet wouldn't face bankruptcy, or worse, because of any health problem.

Hazen, whose reality was excellent insurance and the best care in the world, would never understand that his son couldn't get the same care.

Chapter 17

Mike and Janet visited in November 2004. We took a trip to Catalouchee Valley to photograph the elk herd and the breathtaking landscape there. We used black and white film, shooting a group of elk in front of a barn and mountainscapes from the overlook at the entrance to the valley.

Mike loved the magnificent animals, and he was able to creep up close enough to a young female to shoot a close-up. It was one of his favorite photos. We spent hours shooting black and white and color film—probably a dozen or more rolls.

None of us suspected this would be our last carefree adventure together.

Shortly after Christmas, Mike complained of abdominal pain and constipation, which wasn't supposed to be possible with the way he was hooked up.

His gastroenterologist continued to refuse to give him a colonoscopy without $2,300 cash up front, which Mike didn't have, and Mike still didn't tell Rob and me what was going on.

When we went to visit Mike and Janet in January, Mike was noticeably thinner. He said he'd been having problems but his doctor thought it was chronic constipation. He didn't eat much while we were there; he said it just made him feel sick. He tried to downplay the whole thing, but I could see both he and Janet were worried.

Mike's doctor continued to take a wait-and-see attitude for another couple of weeks. He went to the emergency room and was sent home with pain pills, laxatives, and a bill. Another week went by and this time Mike was told it probably was an ulcer. He went home this time with antibiotics and another bill.

Finally, six weeks after Mike began experiencing pain and constipation, Dr. Patrick Hammen agreed to do a colonoscopy.

Mike came out sooner than Janet expected and they went home to wait for the results. It would be more than a year before we saw the doctor's record: "Couldn't finish procedure. Next time use (pediatric) scope."

Mike's colon was entirely blocked and Dr. Hammen didn't tell him.

In fact, nothing was said until Mike went to see the doctor three weeks later. He was 110 pounds, his kidneys had shut down, and he was vomiting fecal matter.

He called me at work to let me know the doctor was admitting him to the hospital.

My editor at the time, Bob Gabordi, wouldn't even let me finish what I was working on.

"It can wait; your son can't," he said. "Get out of here."

Later that evening, Rob called to tell me I would be paid for any time missed from work and I wouldn't be charged with vacation days. Family is supposed to come before anything else, Bob had said.

I drove the four and a half hours to Savannah and was shocked when I saw Mike. His face was right out of a concentration camp. His eyes were sunken and the skin around them was dark. He was so weak he couldn't sit up for more than a couple of minutes. He had been hours from death before anyone would do anything for him, and it would take five days to stabilize him for surgery.

Next to him on the bed was a tangled mass of blue and red yarn slightly bigger than a football.

"What the hell is that?" I asked.

"It's boo bankie," he said, stroking it. As pieces had unraveled, he had tied them back together, again and again, until the blanket was little more than a ball of knotted yarn.

When Mike found out he had been vomiting fecal matter, he was delighted that he now was the expert on "tastes like shit." For the rest of his life, when he heard someone say something tasted like crap, he would take a taste of the offending substance and shake his head.

"Nope, tastes nothing like it," he said.

Janet and I spent as much time as we could at the hospital, even though she needed to study. Sometimes we sat for hours as Mike slept. I crocheted and she worked on making a hand-stitched skirt.

Danny came when his work schedule permitted, and he brought the kids whenever any of them wanted to come.

One afternoon, he asked if he could switch the TV to *Fox News* and I groaned.

"If it's so bad, why is it the most watched news channel?" Danny asked.

"Because people are sheep," I said.

"No," Mike said, struggling to prop himself up on one elbow.

For a moment, Danny thought he had won the debate.

"People are *fucking* sheep," Mike said, and dropped back down onto the bed, smiling.

The night before surgery, the urologist came to see Mike. He didn't say much other than "see you in surgery," before he got up to leave.

"We have a few questions," I said.

"Well, we don't know what we'll find," he said dismissively.

I stood up, blocking his path.

"This might be a charity case," I said. "But we have questions and I want them answered. If you don't know what you'll find, give us the two or three most likely scenarios."

We stood staring each other down for a moment before he sat again and talked to us. I smiled and thanked him as he rose to leave.

When we returned to the hospital in the morning, Mike was being prepped for surgery. Earlier, tubes had been inserted through his back into his kidneys so the kidneys would drain. Now the tubes were reinforced with hard plastic, and it was excruciatingly painful for him.

Once he was in pre-op, Dr. Hammen ordered pain medication. The nurse stood across the room, continuing to work on paperwork.

After several minutes, I went and asked her to please get Mike the pain medication, and she told me she was busy. It wasn't until

I forced her to watch him writhing in pain and threatened to go find the doctor that she put down her pen and got the medication.

Watching a child go into surgery is frightening no matter what the age. As he was wheeled out of pre-op, a sick feeling crept over me, a rising panic that suggested this might be the last time I saw my son alive. I fought the urge to chase him down the hall. Instead, I stood with Janet for a moment before going back up to his hospital room.

We didn't hear anything for hours—no one came into the room or called us to let us know how he was doing. We decided that meant things must be OK.

As the day dragged on, we asked the nurses on the floor if they could check, and they told us the surgery was going well.

My phone was giving me trouble. No one could figure out why I could make calls only to phones with the same service provider as I had. Janet had a different provider. I made call after call, first to my provider, who said the problem was on the other end, then to Mike and Janet's provider, who said it would take a couple of days to figure it out.

I finally called my provider back and barked into the phone.

"Look, it's not like I'm trying to make a nail appointment," I said. "My son is seriously ill and I need to communicate with my daughter-in-law. Someone, somewhere needs to take responsibility here."

Fortunately, my provider, Verizon, did. Finally, Janet and I felt like we could be apart for a few moments.

When Mike finally came out of surgery I had a hell of a time tracking down Dr. Hammen. I finally caught up with him in the hospital lobby, where he described the surgery. Mike would have a colonostomy, at least for a few months. His kidneys would drain through flexible tubes in his back to urine bags.

The thought that the blockage was cancer still hadn't occurred to me; I was in complete denial.

I stayed in Savannah a few more days to make sure everything was all right. I felt a little uneasy leaving while he was still in the hospital, but I didn't want to take advantage of my boss's generosity, and Mike and Janet assured me they would call if anything came up.

I got the call a few days later as I was in my bedroom getting ready for work. The moment is locked in my brain as I am forced to relive it again and again. I can still hear the panic in his voice every time I replay the moment.

"Mom, I have cancer," Mike said. The words echoed and swam around in my brain. My child has cancer. How can this be? My child isn't supposed to get cancer.

Cancer.

Cancer.

Mike said Dr. Hammen had come in that morning and somewhat dismissively assumed Mike had already heard the results of the pathology report.

"It's a hell of a way to find out you have cancer," he said.

He would have to wait several weeks more for an oncologist to tell him the cancer was stage 3 and that it was signet-ring adenocarcinoma, an aggressive form of cancer usually found in the stomach—the type so often found in people who had the type of surgery he'd had at fifteen months of age.

If he'd been able to get insurance, he could have had the procedure reversed in time to avoid getting cancer, but no insurance company would sell him a policy because he was at such high risk of getting sick.

Of course, Mike was determined to beat the cancer. He told me he talked to it all the time.

"OK, Cancer, listen up. You can't stay here. You have to go. I have plans for my life and they don't include you."

Rob and I went to visit after he had seen the oncologist and had gotten a port in his upper arm for his chemo treatments. His first treatment was a two-week infusion with a portable pump.

"It's a weapon," he told me. "If anybody pisses me off, I can club 'em with the pump."

We wanted to take Mike and Janet out to eat and we decided on an Asian fusion place that they had wanted to try. As he had been doing since his surgery, Mike went out in plaid flannel pajama bottoms and a T-shirt.

The maître d' started to tell us Mike wasn't dressed properly, but Mike showed him the chemo pump.

"I have cancer," he said. "The pants are because the incision from my surgery is still pretty painful."

The maître d' and a waitress who was standing nearby almost fell over themselves getting us a table.

"I call it the cancer card," Mike whispered to us after they walked away. "It's my way of finding something positive in all this."

Mike played the cancer card as often as he could, and it usually worked.

Just before he started chemo, the oncologist told him he needed to be up and moving around—even though he probably wouldn't feel like it.

So, when his chemo started and he felt crappy, he asked Janet to get up and get him a glass of water. She looked up from her art project and said, "You need to be up and moving around. You've been in that chair all day and you know it's not good for you to do that."

Mike struggled to his feet as Janet went back to her work.

"Oh," she said, without looking up again, "while you're up, could you get me a glass of water?"

It was the dreaded reverse cancer card, which Mike would run into time and again from family members and friends.

Although the reverse cancer card was funny, Mike's friends and family were always there for him, as he had been for them.

Mike continued to be active in his twelve-step group, and he made himself available to people who needed help, no matter what time it was. Many times, he got out of bed in the middle of the night to just listen to someone who needed to talk, or to help someone work the steps.

A few months after surgery, Mike called to tell me he had saved someone's life.

James wasn't answering his phone, and Mike knew something was wrong. James had been depressed and Mike was certain he needed help. He drove to James's apartment and let himself in.

"I already had the plastic bag over my head," James told me later. "I had taken the pills and I was ready to die."

Mike got James to the hospital, where his stomach was pumped and he was prescribed antidepressants. For the next three weeks, Mike stayed by James's side. When he came up to visit us, James was with him.

"I hope you don't mind having a crazy person staying at your house," James said one evening.

"Really?" I said. "You think I even notice your brand of crazy? I raised Mike."

"Yeah, I guess that would make you a special kind of crazy," he said.

James would never abandon Mike. In fact, he would become Mike's primary caregiver toward the end of his life. He would more than pay back the favor Mike had extended to him.

Chapter 18

Not long after surgery, Mike and Janet started looking for a new place to live. The mobile home park where they were renting had become less and less safe. While Mike was in the hospital, someone had broken into the house and stolen their camera equipment.

Their next door neighbor had split their cable signal so he didn't have to pay for cable. Mike caught him and reported it, which didn't endear him to the neighbor.

During the summer after Mike's surgery, they found a new place near downtown Savannah, a rambling old Victorian house with a small yard in a neighborhood that was largely students from the Savannah College of Art and Design.

The street was lined with old oak trees draped in Spanish moss. As majestic as the neighborhood seemed, though, it wasn't ideal; nothing could be left outdoors.

"I caught some asshole trying to steal my lawnmower," Mike said about a month after they moved in. "He was just walking down the street with it when I caught him."

I bought plastic Adirondack chairs for the front porch so they wouldn't have to sit on the steps, but the chairs didn't last the weekend.

"If you leave anything outside, some asshole will figure it's your gift to him," Mike said.

The afternoon that Mike finished chemo, he called me to tell me he was done. I was with my friend, Bill Jamieson, an Episcopalian deacon and director of Servanthood House, and we said a prayer of thanks. Although Bill hadn't met Mike, he had been following Mike's progress through our "liberal lunches," meetings where we bemoaned the lack of compassion in governmental policies.

A common topic during these lunches was health care policy. Bill had worked in government in Arizona during the Bruce Babbitt administration and in Washington, DC, under Jimmy Carter, on children's welfare policy.

"All we did in public policy, in making laws to benefit children's health and well-being, was dismantled by the next administration," he told me.

"If we can't change things by passing laws, what hope is there?" I asked. "What can we do?"

"We can do what Jesus did," he said. "We can tell stories."

As a newspaper reporter, that was my job, and I had won a number of awards for telling the stories of real people to illustrate the impact of government policies. I had won awards and changed state policy.

I had changed the way CAP MR-DD was administered.

When I covered the state's mental health "reform," I found people who were affected by all the changes and told their stories.

When the state started talking about closing centers that employ people with disabilities and letting them find jobs in the private sector, I wrote a story. I interviewed a young man who was able to live on his own with help from family and neighbors because of the job he had. I interviewed parents of another person who both worked and needed their daughter to be in the workshop during the day. In rural areas, there weren't jobs for people with disabilities, and most of the people who worked in employment centers would be out of work.

By noon on the day the story was published, the state had heard from more than six hundred people. The plan to close the centers was shelved permanently.

The investigative work I did helped people get and keep the services they needed, and I was immensely proud of that. But I saw that, all too often, people who managed to get their stories into the paper or onto television were the only ones who got the help they needed.

A woman who needed a wheelchair ramp had been homebound for five years, but as soon as her story was in the paper, she got the ramp built.

I have been a storyteller all my life, but I couldn't tell the stories of all the people who were raising money for medical bills with donations in coffee cans on convenience store counters. Too many of them were dying because they couldn't get the publicity they needed to raise the money for care.

In September of 2005, my older sister, Ellen, was diagnosed with lung cancer. She called me the night before surgery to say they had found "something nasty" on her lung and she was going in to have it removed. With a little prodding, she admitted it was cancer.

"I don't want any drama," she said. "I just want to get it taken out and go on from there."

My mother was convinced that God would cure Ellen and everything would be fine. Ellen vowed to fight it. The rest of us knew the battle wasn't likely to be successful, but we were willing to hope.

Mike was having trouble keeping food down again. He was starting to lose weight. The oncologists told him he might have adhesions in his abdomen from all the surgeries he'd had, or that there was a possibility the radiation was causing some obstruction in his small intestine. They wanted to take a wait-and-see approach.

When Shannon called to tell me the doctors found a larger tumor on Ellen's lung than they had hoped, I fell apart. Anything larger than a dime is usually fatal, and Ellen's tumor was the size of a golf ball.

Mike was sick again and Ellen was dying. I had made three errors in stories in the span of a week. Instead of telling me I should take time off, my bosses put me on probation and threatened to fire me. Bob Gabordi was gone, transferred to a newspaper in Florida, and the people now in charge only thought about the paper and not the people who worked to produce it.

I took a few days off and went to the doctor, who put me on antidepressants again.

I went to visit Mike and Janet again in October. While I was there, I took Mike grocery shopping. He had applied for disability but hadn't received word yet.

As we were checking out, he asked for a candy bar. "Oh, Mommy, please?" he said.

"No," I answered. "You need to be eating nutritious food."

"But . . ." He hesitated for a moment. "But I have *cancer!* I might *die!*"

The checkout clerk and the woman behind me in line glared at me.

"Cancer, *schmancer*," I said, getting out my cash and staring them both down. "I am so tired of hearing about that."

As we got out into the parking lot, Mike doubled over laughing. "Oh that was so fuckin' funny," he said. "Let's go back in and check out again."

"I can't ever go in there again," I said. "I'd be lynched."

It was another way of playing the cancer card. He would shock people and make me look bad if I would go along with it. I went along.

Within a couple of weeks, it was obvious the situation wasn't going to correct itself. He was losing weight quickly. He and I had planned to go to Massachusetts to see Ellen around our birthday, but he was too sick to go.

So, for our annual anniversary trip, Rob and I went to Savannah.

Once again, we were shocked to see how sick Mike looked. The doctors were still waiting to see if the situation would correct itself while Mike was starving and in constant pain.

We spent three days in Savannah, most of it hanging out with Mike and watching TV.

"This is what I'm reduced to," he said when *Family Feud* came on.

While we were there, Mike celebrated his ninth sobriety anniversary. He asked me to attend the meeting and give him the nine-year chip.

When we arrived, Robin G., who was setting up the room, asked Mike to set out the literature on a back table.

"But, I have *cancer*," he said.

"That shouldn't prevent you from setting out the literature," she said.

When it came time to hand Mike the nine-year chip, I was asked to say a few words—something I rarely turn down.

"You were a tough kid," I said. "You were even tougher as a teenager. A lot of people gave up on you. I was tempted to do so myself. But you woke up. You worked on yourself and you have become an amazing man. I am so proud of the man you have become, and I'm proud to be your mom."

On our last day there, we decided to go to Tybee Island and watch a sunset.

As the sun sank, Mike sighed. "I love my life," he said.

He was in constant pain and starving, but he still was able to see the beauty around him and appreciate the people who loved him. As always, he found joy, no matter how dire his circumstances.

After we went home, Mike went to the doctor again, and a few days before Thanksgiving they admitted him to the hospital for tests. I went down, and as he seemed to have improved and was released Thursday morning, I went home for Thanksgiving. We were planning on having the whole family at our house for a Friday dinner. But on Thursday night, Mike was admitted to the hospital again.

I cooked for Danny and Jennifer and the kids, but left again on Saturday to be with Mike. By now he was down to 104 pounds and they weren't feeding him intravenously. The doctor on call said since Dr. Hammen was out of town, he didn't want to take responsibility because Mike might have an insulin reaction.

"Well, he's in the right place if there's an emergency, isn't he?" Janet asked.

The doctor wasn't going to do anything.

"Well then," I said. "Maybe it's time to take this to the media."

"What do you know about the media?" the doctor asked.

"I AM the media," I said. "I have been a reporter for more than twenty-five years and I know just the words to use to get attention. Something like 'deliberate starvation of a thirty-one-year-old man because he doesn't have insurance,' ought to have print and broadcast media at the door. Maybe you'd like to explain that to your bosses."

Mike got the IV nutrition he needed within a few minutes.

Dr. Hammen came back a couple of days later and blamed the oncologists for letting Mike get so sick. He would perform surgery as soon as Mike was stable.

Hazen came up from Brunswick to sit with Janet and me while Mike was in surgery. Mike had made Janet promise to finish school, no matter what, before he went into the operating room.

"He should never have gotten this malnourished," Dr. Hammen told me before surgery. "He's at much higher risk because of it."

Surgery went on most of the day, and Mike made it through. They resected the small intestine, which had been damaged by radiation, and now it was just a matter of waiting for the pathology report and getting some weight onto Mike's bones.

We saw him briefly, and then went to dinner.

Hazen talked about his cancer and how he knew Mike would be OK.

"I survived it, so can he," he said.

Radiation had taken its toll on Hazen, too. It had damaged his spine and left him unable to walk without braces and a walker. He should have gotten a power chair, but he was stubborn and he wanted to walk.

"It damaged my testicles, too," he said. "I didn't know that until I started to grow boobs, so now I'm on hormone replacement therapy."

"Well, you always were a breast man," I said.

Janet groaned. "This is more than I need—or want—to know," she said.

Mike slept most of the next day, with Janet, Hazen, and me in the room. At one point, I was alone in the room with him. I was working on a scarf—I was crocheting one or two a day to work off nervous energy. I looked over at him sleeping, and I knew this scene would be repeated, except he would be dying then. I tried to shake it off, but it wouldn't go away.

I would watch my son die.

Chapter 19

The second day after surgery, Mike was awake and alert. I had told Janet to sleep late and run some errands before she went to the hospital.

"I want her here," Mike said. "I hate to be alone."

"You're not alone," I said. "Your dad and I are here."

He called Janet and laid on the guilt. Here he was, one day out of surgery, blah, blah, blah. Janet hung up on him.

"You need to call her back and apologize," I said. "She and I spent the last forty-eight hours here and she had some things she needed to get done."

"No, I had surgery yesterday," he said.

"No, you had surgery the day before yesterday," I said.

"I hate to hear myself say this," Hazen interrupted, "but your mother's right."

It took us a minute to convince him he had lost an entire day, and when he realized he was right, he called Janet back to apologize.

The next day he was out of bed, walking slowly, and wheeling along his IV pole. He and Hazen were "racing" around the hospital floor at a snail's pace.

The following day, Mike was walking in the corridor when I arrived. He looked awful.

"Mom, they found more cancer," he said.

I thought my knees would buckle, but I got him back into bed and went and found Dr. Hammen.

The pathology report had found "a few viable cells," he said.

"Well couldn't you remove them?" I asked. "His dad had a metastasis on his lung and they removed it and he's been fine for four years."

"Oh, we wouldn't do that," he said.

"Well, then, fuck you!"

I stalked back into Mike's room and the doctor followed me in.

"I wouldn't be offended if you wanted to seek another opinion," he said.

I was about to jump down his throat when Janet stood up. "Excuse me," she said.

Janet had this.

She moved toward Hammen. "I was just sitting here thinking I would like to save my husband's life, but not at the cost of offending you," she said. She poked him in the chest and continued talking. "After all, your feelings are our most important consideration here."

He took a step back and mentioned that we might try "a little chemotherapy," but that Mike should get his affairs in order.

Janet poked some more, giving him hell as he backed out of the room.

Mike was in the hospital nine more days and not one doctor stopped in to talk to him during that time. The day he was discharged he received a note from the oncology clinic saying he should call in a few weeks.

I started calling cancer care centers all over the eastern half of the country. They kept telling me they were overflowing with patients who couldn't pay and they couldn't accept any more.

I knew that was true because I had spent more than a quarter century writing about health policy. If you could get your story on the news or in the paper, people might donate enough to help you get started on chemo. The stories were enough to tear at my heart and keep me awake nights wondering what more I could do for people. And now, here I was, unable to find help for my son. I knew the system as well as anyone—and better than most—but I couldn't get him the help he needed.

Finally, someone at Duke University Medical Center said we could pay for a consultation with Dr. Herbert Hurwitz. It would be about $400. We made the appointment.

Just over six weeks post-surgery, we went to Duke. Mike's incision was weeping a foul-smelling discharge and he was changing his dressing every half hour or so.

When Dr. Hurwitz looked at the incision, he asked Mike when he last saw his surgeon.

"A few days ago," Mike said. "He told me I'm healing slowly because I was so malnourished going in."

It turned out Mike had a life-threatening infection in his surgical incision. Either Dr. Hammen was incompetent or he was planning to just let Mike die from the infection. This was the second time Dr. Hammen had failed to inform Mike of a life-threatening condition.

"Duke will adopt you," Dr. Hurwitz said. "You'll need Medicaid to pay for the chemo, but we'll take care of you."

He ordered a scan, and the radiology department said he would have to pay for it out of pocket. Dr. Hurwitz told them to do the scan without demanding payment, and it was done.

Finally, we had an ally who cared more about Mike's life than his own pocketbook.

Mike finished the first round of the antibiotic, which had cost several hundred dollars, and he needed a second round. I was getting close to the limit on my credit cards and his Medicaid hadn't been approved yet.

I had an appointment to speak to Bill Murdock, director of Eblen Charities—a nonprofit that helps people get money for medications and pays for gasoline so people can travel to medical appointments. I was going to write a story about a fund-raiser.

"You know we're here," Bill told me when I told him all that was going on with Mike. "Why don't you and Mike come and see me tomorrow?"

Mike and Bill are pretty similar people. Both of them could do several things at once. Mike noticed Bill had two computer monitors and then affirmed his belief that he should have three.

"I have three," Mike said. "You can get a lot more done." The next time I dropped in to see Bill, he had three monitors.

Bill sent payment for Mike's antibiotic to the pharmacy and then gave him a voucher for a tank of gas so he could drive to Durham for his next appointment, which likely would be covered by Medicaid.

When Mike had applied for Medicaid, he was told he and Janet would have to separate for him to get it. He gave my address as his home address and I had to write a letter saying they were separated and not planning on getting back together.

That may have been my most brokenhearted moment. My son had to end his marriage to have any hope of beating cancer. It was inhumane.

I wrote a letter that didn't state categorically that they would stay separated, and a social worker called me and said the letter had to state as a matter of fact that I believed the split was permanent.

#

Mike spent some of his time with me, but most of his days were spent in Savannah with Janet. I lived in fear that they would be discovered and that he would lose Medicaid—his only hope of receiving the care he needed.

Duke is four hours from Asheville and six hours from Savannah, but Shannon and Matt were living in Fayetteville, just over an hour away from the medical center. Mike could go there and Shannon or Matt would bring him to chemo, wait three or four hours for him to finish, and drive him back to Fayetteville.

In mid-January, I was making my annual winter trip to New Jersey and Massachusetts, and Mike decided he wanted to come. Ellen was in the middle of chemo, and he wanted to see her.

In New Jersey, our entire group of friends goes out to dinner at LuCa's, an upscale Italian restaurant. The adult children would come along and we've had as many as twenty-three in the party. This year we had eighteen and they put us in a private room that was barely big enough to seat all of us.

For Mike, it was a homecoming. He had grown up with all these people and they were his extended family. Most had been at his wedding and he hadn't seen many of them since.

He had put on about fifteen pounds since surgery—he had weighed 104 pounds when he was admitted to the hospital—and was eating ravenously. Breakfast was an instant breakfast mixed with ice cream, heavy cream, an egg, and regular milk—with a little extra chocolate sauce thrown in. He had another one of those before bed at night.

In Massachusetts, we stayed at Ellen's house. She was doing pretty well, although there was still some deep bone pain from the chemo.

"I looked for a survivors' group for this," Ellen told me. "There aren't any. It seems hardly anybody survives."

We still hoped she might be one of the few. She was still bald from the effects of chemo, but it was more a source of humor than sympathy.

"Oh my God, do you have any idea how much you look like Daddy?" I asked when she removed her head scarf.

"I own mirrors," she said.

The family Christmas party was a little too much for Mike, who went upstairs and took a nap after the gift exchange. He had little tolerance for commotion, even though he usually had been the biggest cause of it. He was still weak, and he had a chemo appointment a few days after we got back.

\#

I wound up with a Thomas Kinkade "collectible" teacup and saucer. It amused the hell out of Mike because Ellen was the one who loved Kinkade. I never did. In fact, I couldn't stand him. Mike couldn't wait to call Danny and tell him.

When we got back, Danny came up from Georgia so the three of us could spend a few days together. Every time I entered a room, the teacup and saucer were there, propped up by a handy stand for optimum viewing.

I tried to ignore it, but it was funny to find it moved a dozen times a day, as if by elves. I could hear the two of them laughing whenever I walked into the room where they had placed it.

In the end, I just left it where they put it. When they left, it was on the TV stand and that's where it sits today in all its dusty glory.

#

The first evening we were all together, Mike sat us down.

"We need to talk," he said. "There's the possibility this won't be cured."

Danny didn't want to talk about the possibility of Mike dying, but Mike made us listen. He told us what he wanted—no life-prolonging measures unless there was a chance for him to have a good quality of life, which wouldn't be likely.

"I don't intend to let this get me, but I might not have control over that," he said.

The possibility that he would die from this was real, and he balked at making any long-range plans. Janet wanted him to go back to school, but he refused.

"I don't want to spend time in school right now," he told me. "I love to work with my hands, and I want to do that for awhile."

When he felt up to it, he was able to work with a friend who did odd jobs in painting and construction. Between his near death from malnutrition and the chemo, he wasn't able to do much.

Chapter 20

Mike loved spending a couple of days every other week with Shannon. He got to play video games with Matt and pretend to be a dog when he was playing with their three-year-old daughter, Cassie. She was shy, but when Cousin Mike barked, she squealed with delight.

During Mike's chemo, Shannon announced she was pregnant, due in late October. She continued to drive him to and from his appointments, with an often cranky Cassie in tow.

Ellen had finished her chemo and was taking walks and hoping to get back to work. She was eager to see her third grandchild. She and KJ had gotten married in February so if decisions needed to be made, KJ would be the one with the legal authority to do so. They were fortunate enough to live in Massachusetts, the first state to grant marriage equality.

But in early May, cancer was found in Ellen's liver. It no longer was a question of whether she would survive, but of how long she would have—and whether she would live to see her grandson born.

Rob and I were on our way to visit his brother in Louisville, and we had tickets to an afternoon at the races at Churchill Downs, when Mike called. I only heard the words "cancer" and "liver," and I thought it was his liver and his cancer. I began to panic as he spoke, until I heard him say "Ellen." It didn't make me feel better. We had tried so hard to believe Ellen could beat this.

When I talked to her, she told me she knew this was going to kill her.

"Maybe, I said, "but not today."

"Damn right," she said. "Every day above ground is a good day."

The cancer also was invading her brain and she was becoming increasingly forgetful. We talked more frequently because we both knew our time was limited.

Rob and I went to visit in early July for the annual family summer get-together. Mike came with Danny and Jennifer and the kids. We all knew this likely would be Ellen's last family party. This one was at my sister Robin's home in southern New Hampshire.

It was obvious that Ellen was very ill. The steroids that helped her breathe bloated her face. She was using a cane to walk because she was having hip pain, and she was as forgetful as a mid-stage Alzheimer's patient.

Our mother held out hope that God would perform a miracle and save Ellen's life. But the rest of us knew better.

As Robin's husband, Tim, finished the first round of burgers and dogs, he called out for the kids to go first. Mike grabbed Ellen and they made their way to the table.

"I said kids first," Tim said as Mike handed an empty plate to Ellen.

"We have cancer," Mike said, gesturing to himself and Ellen.

"Mine's inoperable," Ellen chirped, grinning.

They laughed at their success at getting first dibs on the food, slapped a high five, and filled their plates.

The next day, at Ellen's house, she and Rob and I sat out on the deck in the sun. Rob brought out a beer and Ellen went to grab one for herself.

"Don't tell Katherine," she said. "She doesn't want me to drink, but I love beer and I want one."

She sat down at the table and pulled a cigarette and lighter out of her pocket.

"Are you sure you want to do that?" Rob asked.

"I think that horse has left the barn already," Ellen said.

The next day, I took Ellen for an X-ray of her hip. Neither one of us wanted to say what we knew would be the result: that the cancer had invaded her bones. Afterward, we went to the Cape Cod Canal, where Ellen and KJ had a camper. We walked along the canal and went to have lunch at Seafood Sam's, right across the Bourne Bridge on Cape Cod.

"You know, people keep telling me I'm a hero," Ellen said. "I don't feel like a hero. I think I'm just somebody dealing with something in the best way I can. I always say 'thank you,' but it makes me uncomfortable to be a hero."

On my last full day there, we took Rob on a tour of Sheldonville, the little village where we spent our formative years on an apple farm.

The orchard itself is a housing development and the meadows are neatly mowed yards. The pasture pine where we used to sit in the shade on sultry summer days and read is gone. We pointed out where the Cowley family had its dog kennel and where the cranberry bog was before somebody removed the dam.

We passed the Wheelers' dairy farm, now a town park, and where the Nolans' house had been. There was Robert Dresser's house. He was a millionaire businessman and a member of the John Birch Society. And the Hemmingsens, whose parents told us we could call them Joan and Bob; our parents nipped that one in the bud.

Darcy Omen had been on the TV talent show *Community Auditions*, which was sponsored by Community Opticians: "Star of the day, who will it be? Your vote will hold the key . . ." She danced in a sailor suit and we thought it was fabulous, but she didn't win. Still, she was on TV and that was huge.

The Browns' house looked better than it did when we were kids. Mrs. Brown would pass out on the couch pretty early in the day, her empty scotch glass on the coffee table. Our parents always wanted the kids to come to our house to play so they could be supervised.

There was the Sheldonville Baptist Church, where we learned that women were inferior to men and that lesbians and gays were all going to burn in hell. Fortunately, we unlearned that later.

We passed the Stewarts' house, which had burned to the ground and had been rebuilt with the help of neighbors. The Sheldons' house was still standing, although we didn't know if it was still in the family.

The Presleys had a little girl with developmental disabilities and they had the courage to keep her at home instead of institutionalizing her. She was often playing in the yard when the school bus came by. Children with disabilities had no right to an education then.

The general store/post office/hair salon/ insurance agency was still open, and still had room for a half dozen cars in the parking lot.

We went home the back way so we could stop at The Ice Cream Machine in Cumberland, Rhode Island, and get triple-scoop hot fudge sundaes for lunch.

It was the best, most intense visit Ellen and I ever had, and I knew it likely would be the last.

A few days later, Ellen and I were talking on the phone and she told me she had lost her cigarettes. "If Katherine finds them, she'll be so mad," Ellen said. "What would I even say?"

"Simple," I answered. "Just tell her you don't remember putting them there."

"Damn! I hope I can remember that," she said, laughing.

Two weeks after we saw her, she went into the hospital because she was having trouble breathing. The doctors discovered a large tumor that was almost blocking her airway. Ellen knew she wasn't going to beat lung cancer, but she desperately wanted to live to see her grandson born. She asked if there was anything left to do and her doctor said there was a powerful chemo regimen that might give her a little more time.

"Good," she said. "I have a way I can keep fighting."

But the chemo caused blood clots in her lungs. Knowing how desperately Ellen wanted just three more months, KJ agreed to a respirator that would keep Ellen breathing until the clots had a chance to clear out. It was a long shot, but we all knew Ellen would want to try.

I got a call from my niece, Christina, telling me it was time to come to Massachusetts.

I arrived on July 24. Ellen was being kept sedated, but her heart rate would go up when she heard a new, familiar voice. I told her I'd heard there was a party so I came right up because God knows I don't want to miss a family party. I sat by her bed and crocheted for awhile. Her son and daughter-in-law stopped in and we talked about the lace bedspread she was making for Shannon.

Ellen loved to crochet, but she wasn't as fond of putting the pieces together. My nephew told me he had seen bags full of the 4-inch pieces all crocheted and waiting to be put together.

"I think we might be able to make a house cozy with it," he joked.

Ellen and I had always debated the best way to piece projects together. She insisted they should be sewn together using a darning needle and I stuck with my firm opinion that they should be crocheted together.

I know she heard us discussing this, and I know she wanted KJ to give the bedspread pieces to someone else to assemble.

I left late in the evening to stay with my stepmother. I received a call in the middle of the night that the end seemed near. I rushed over to the hospital and sat next to Ellen. The crisis had passed, but we knew the respirator wasn't working and she probably had no more than a matter of hours. I wanted to say good-bye now.

"I want you to know I'll think of you every day," I started. "And when you see Daddy, tell him I miss him. I really believe I'll see you again—unless you see me first. I love you. I'll miss you. Just so you know."

I went back to Barbara's house and was awakened at seven by another call. This was it. But by the time I got to the hospital, she was gone.

The doctor told KJ and Shannon and Stephen what they already knew: Ellen wasn't responding to treatment. It was time to let go.

KJ leaned over the bed.

"E, I know you wanted to live to see Liam born, but you're just going to have to see it from Heaven."

Peace came across Ellen's face; she snorted loudly and left everyone laughing.

\#

My mother had believed right to the end that Ellen would survive. She had a prayer chain going at church and she had convinced herself that Ellen would be OK. Now she just fell apart, wandering her house and alternating between sobbing and wailing. Sedatives were the only things that helped.

My mother's pastor, an Evangelical Christian, presided at Ellen's funeral. Pastor Dan Dore had been upset when Ellen and KJ eloped. He had wanted to be the one to officiate at their wedding. He knew he was expected to be against marriage equality, but he was a staunch supporter.

"God doesn't make mistakes," he said. "The extravagant love that Ellen and KJ shared can only come from God, so I know it was God-given."

He talked about Ellen's sense of humor and about how she and KJ took in three children whose parents couldn't raise them and raised them as their own.

I wish there had been more time for funny stories about Ellen, but we would share those afterward and for years to come.

Chapter 21

Shannon was due to deliver the end of October, and Mike was getting increasingly nervous that Liam might come on his birthday, which he already had to share with me.

"Don't drop that kid on my birthday," Mike warned again and again. "I already have to share it with one person; I don't want to share it with anybody else!"

On November 2, the day before Mike's and my birthday, Shannon gave birth to Liam (William Gerard). He weighed in at just over ten pounds. When Shannon brought him home, she noticed a toad sitting on the deck, watching her every move. The toad was there for several days, always right up against the sliding door, always watching.

"It's Mom," she said. "I know it's Mom."

I went to visit a few days after he was born and bonded a little with him and Cassie. I figure it's up to me to tell Shannon's kids about their grandmother so they'll at least know who she was. They call me "Auntie." No name other than that is necessary because they know who they're talking about, even though they have several other aunts. They also know their mom and I laugh a lot whenever we get together.

Shannon had decided to go back to school to become an RN, and Matt would soon be deployed to Qatar in the Middle East. Life was about to get even more hectic for her. Still, she always had time to take care of Mike when he needed it.

In September, KJ gave me an unfinished crochet lace tablecloth that Ellen had been working on and asked if I thought I could finish it. I took it home with me and began putting together the pieces she had crocheted already, using my own method: the crochet hook.

That night, Ellen came to me in a dream. She stood in front of me, hands on her hips and scolded, "It's my project, dammit! Use the darning needle!"

No one will ever convince me that wasn't Ellen. I started using the darning needle.

It was the night before Thanksgiving when Ellen's death really hit me hard. I was on my way home from work when I realized that I couldn't call her to discuss our Thanksgiving menus.

"I'm cooking for sixteen," she would say. "How many you got?"

"Only seven."

This was Ellen's season. From Thanksgiving until mid-January, she was in high gear. Her house was decorated from top to bottom—dozens of Father Christmas figures—from a few inches to three feet tall—a Christmas village that took up half of the dining room, and a huge Christmas tree that occupied about a third of the living room.

Talking to Ellen about what we were making for the big meal was almost as much of a tradition as the meal itself.

Rob got home about nine, just as I was about to pop an apple pie into the oven.

"How's it going?" he asked.

I looked at him, fully intending to say, "OK," but instead I burst into tears.

"I miss my sister," I wailed.

I have a talent for doing fine and then just falling apart all of a sudden, when everyone—including me—least expects it. After my father died, the trigger was my inability to find the book, *The Velveteen Rabbit*, which my father had read to me as a child. I was in hysterics when Rob suggested this might be about my father. I continued sobbing and insisted it was about the book.

But this was about Ellen. It was the volcano of emotion that had been building since she was diagnosed with lung cancer. I'm not a weeper; I just wait until I burst out into uncontrollable wailing.

I wanted to hear what Ellen was cooking. I wanted to hear about her Christmas decorations, which would be brought out the day after Thanksgiving. I longed to hear what new things she had bought to expand the Christmas village in her dining room, and what new Father Christmas figure she had found at the Christmas Store on Cape Cod.

Right around Christmas, I dreamed about Ellen again. We were in her living room and she was sitting on the couch. I called her name and she sat bolt upright, grinning.

"You can see me? You can hear me?" she asked excitedly.

"Yeah. What are you doing here?

"Katherine still needs me," she said. "I'll go when I know she's OK."

She was bored, she said, since nobody could see or hear her. She and I always had a strong—I guess you could call it psychic—connection. She often answered questions I hadn't asked out loud yet; I often knew what she was up to before she said anything.

The annual family winter party was in the middle of January, and Shannon and the kids and I all stayed at the house. We weren't there an hour before Shannon took me aside.

"Mom's still here, isn't she?" Shannon said. "I can feel her presence."

I told her what Ellen had told me.

In February of 2007, Ellen visited me one final time. In the dream, I had just finished throwing a huge party and I was starting to clean up. She appeared next to me and we started working together and laughing. A friend came into the room and I introduced him.

"I thought she was dead," he said.

"Oh, I am dead," Ellen said, grinning, "but I'm always here if you need me."

I have sensed her presence many times. I swear I've heard her laugh when something stupid happens and I feel as though I'm the butt of yet another of her practical jokes.

#

I was tired most of the time, probably from the stress of working and worrying about Mike.

Being a reporter at a daily newspaper was getting increasingly difficult. Small tasks were added to our day again and again with the excuse, "it'll only take five minutes," until there were no more "five minutes" in the day, and the company wasn't offering any overtime. Newsroom clerical assistant jobs were being cut and reporters and editors were being told to take up the slack.

The news stories that I knew needed to be told were being set aside so I could do more short, snappy features. I was trying to make time for an investigation of a group of homes that housed people with mental illnesses and developmental disabilities. I had heard of people wandering off because of a lack of supervision, of medications not being given at the proper time, thefts, and more.

I tried to convince editors that we needed to look into this but was told I would have to do it "in snippets." You don't do investigative work in snippets; you take the time to do research and find credible sources who will go on the record.

Ultimately, an elderly man wandered off from one of these homes and later was found dead. I felt as though his life could have been saved if I had taken the time to do the investigation, even on my own time.

The job was becoming something other than what I had signed on for some twenty-five years earlier. We were putting tits-and-ass photos up on our website under the guise of bikini fashion shows because they got hits. Everything was about hits, not about explaining public policy to readers. We were out to win popularity, not to inform people. We were told to present "both sides" of a story, even when the supposed other side was nothing more than a lie. Belief was being given as much credibility as science.

I was frustrated at the lack of time to do the important work, of having serious social justice issues trivialized.

I did insist on covering the mental health system, and because the coverage won awards, I was given the go-ahead to work on it. I was the one reporter in the state who fully understood the mental health system and the changes that had nearly destroyed it. It was in a constant state of crisis and no one else was covering it. Beds had been severely reduced at state psychiatric hospitals, and state "area programs," where people could get treatment and case management, were shut down to privatize the system.

My "tour guide" through the system, which also included substance abuse services and services for people with developmental disabilities, was Larry Thompson, formerly head of the area program in Asheville. He was the one who predicted before the system changed over that it would be a train wreck, and he had been right.

When asked about the changes that were coming, people from the state spoke in unintelligible jargon as the public became increasingly frustrated.

The state allowed no time for a private system to be brought up before it closed the area programs, and thousands of people were falling through the cracks. Local emergency rooms were overwhelmed with people in crisis; many were shuttled to jails, and some died.

Services were spun off into nonprofits. Everyone who left the area programs and went to work for the nonprofits lost their state pensions. Many of the big nonprofits closed within a year or two, leaving people with nowhere to go for treatment.

It taught me that when government officials talk about "increasing patient choices," or "enhancing services," it really translates into leaving people with nothing.

It was exactly what Mike had faced in Savannah when he couldn't get care because he didn't have insurance. It was the free market at its worst.

In the new, "reformed" system, no two providers had the same forms for services, so Medicaid workers had to sort through hundreds of different forms for the same information. There was no statewide computer system that connected the one hundred county departments of social services, so people who moved from one county to another often got lost in the system.

Covering this mess was stressful, even though I loved exposing the incompetence at the state level. I made frequent trips to Raleigh to search records or attend legislative meetings. Even though the paper had a reporter in Raleigh, I was the only one who understood the entire mess.

So, I was thrilled when Mike and Janet announced they would move to Raleigh when Janet graduated. They wanted to be near Duke Medical Center and they wanted to live in a city in the

South. Both of them detested cold weather and snow. Mike rarely even uttered the word "snow" without "fuckin'" in front of it.

I was excited that I would be able to see them whenever I went to Raleigh. I realized they likely would only have one bedroom, but I was happy to sleep on a futon or a recliner, and the paper's editors were happy that they wouldn't have to pay for a hotel room every month or so.

In March, Mike called to tell me he and Janet would separate. They both would move to Raleigh, but would be living separately. Janet described it as pretense becoming reality. They had been having difficulty because Mike refused to make any long-range plans, and Janet wanted him to go back to school, to plan as though he would beat the cancer. Mike couldn't bring himself to do that yet and he wasn't certain he ever would be able to do it.

Mike's friend James decided he would move to Raleigh and get an apartment with Mike so that if the cancer came back and Mike wasn't able to work, he could take care of the bills. Their relationship was that of close brothers. They understood each other—they both had the same twisted sense of humor and they both loved working on computers. They began to build computers from spare parts to give to people who were newly sober and trying to get on their feet.

Mike had two stents in his back, which allowed his kidneys to drain directly through tubes into two "pee bags," as Mike and James called them. Mike often threatened to slap people with the bags and then laughed at their reactions.

The stents had bandages around them to keep them clean, and the bandages had to be changed every few days. James was so adept at it that no one else was allowed to do it.

"He knows how to do it without hurting me," Mike said.

Janet found an apartment in Durham, close to the medical center. Mike and James moved to Cary, about a half hour from Durham but closer to James's new job.

The apartment had all the masculine touches—bed sheets tacked to the wall above the windows for curtains, bicycles in the kitchen, a big-screen TV, stereo speakers, and a couch in the living room. Because Mike was a great cook, the kitchen was pretty complete, but clean dishes usually stayed in the dish rack until it was empty, which meant it was time to do the dishes.

It was clean enough so there were no foul smells.

Before moving to Cary, Mike brought me back my Guild nylon string guitar, which I had given him for Christmas the year we moved to Asheville. He had always loved the guitar, and I had stopped playing it. Now he was returning it.

"I don't have room to store it in the new place," he said.

I'm not sure I believed him, as much as I wanted to. I knew, even though I couldn't admit it, that he suspected the cancer would come back.

Chapter 22

In the fall of 2007, Mike started having abdominal pain again. His scans didn't show any cancer, so the doctors assumed the pain was coming from all the invasive surgeries he'd had.

But the pain kept getting worse, and Mike was easily fatigued—a natural response to all he had been through. We talked him into spending Thanksgiving with us, even though he would have preferred to cook for people in his twelve-step group who had nowhere to go for the holiday.

Mike arrived late the night before Thanksgiving, exhausted but thrilled to hear I was making traditional bread stuffing and chocolate cream pie. This was his favorite holiday because it was about gratitude and food. Christmas, on the other hand, was all about stuff. Working in the mall that one year had cured him of ever loving Christmas again.

He spent the rest of the evening picking at things I was trying to prepare for the dinner.

We also invited my friend, Liz Huesemann, director of a local nonprofit that works with people who have developmental and other disabilities. She and Mike hit it off immediately. She started admiring a face jug in the living room and Mike offered it to her.

"Take what you want," he said. "You're the guest. I'll get a box and help you carry it all to the car."

Liz has a large collection of face jugs; I had one, but Mike assured her she was welcome to it again and again during the afternoon.

Much of the afternoon was spent with Liz pointing to things and saying, "Ooh, I like that," and Mike adding it to the list. The joke didn't get old, which is one of the reasons I love Liz. Like Mike, she can drag a joke on and on, long after anyone else thinks it's funny, but she and I will still laugh at it.

Seven years later, she still insists Mike wants her to have the jug.

"He comes to me in dreams and tells me he wants me to have it," she says. "I think he's starting to get upset because you won't give it to me."

Mike was tired after dinner and went to take a nap.

He had been working in a chain restaurant, but he had trouble working a full eight-hour shift. By Christmas, his boss had stopped putting him on the schedule. We were still waiting for his disability to be approved.

With no money coming in, Mike had to rely on family and friends to pay his bills. James explained the dilemma to his boss, who immediately gave him a raise to help cover expenses. Danny and I paid his phone bills. I bought him groceries, clothes, tires—whatever he needed that wasn't already being provided by James.

Hazen wasn't contributing because he didn't realize what dire financial straits Mike was in. The previous year, Hazen had lent Mike some money, but it came with a lecture about paying it back. Mike never told him how tight things were, and he never asked his father for more money.

The cable was still in Mike's name, but James took over paying it. Rob gave him a gasoline credit card. Danny bought him new shoes.

When his tires needed to be replaced, I took Mike to the tire store, and when it came time to pay, Mike opened his empty wallet and turned it so I could see it.

It was time to play "Cancer Card."

"Oh, I get it," I said. "Mommy has to pay for the tires." I pulled out my debit card.

"Well, I would love to pay for them, but it's been kinda hard to come up with any money since I can't work because I have *cancer!*" he said.

The clerk started shuffling his feet uncomfortably until Mike started laughing.

"I'm sorry," he said. "I don't have a lot of pleasures left to me, but I can still laugh."

The clerk joined in and thanked us for coming in and making his day.

Mike was losing weight, and he was having trouble eating. James was buying whatever he thought Mike would eat, which included bagels, cornflakes, chocolate, and coffee. He made high-calorie milkshakes in hopes that Mike would drink a whole one.

In early February, Cadbury Crème Eggs started appearing in the stores, and James bought them by the case because they were Mike's favorite candy. It was something Mike would eat, and James kept buying them.

Mike was planning to come out for a weekend in February, but he was feeling so sick, he asked that I come visit him instead. It was an easy drive—a straight shot across I-40 from Exit 44 to Exit 297 with less than two miles of off-highway driving at either end.

On February 18, I was interviewing a couple who own a chocolate shop in Asheville. They were donating a portion of their proceeds to a domestic violence agency and I was doing a story on them.

I never turned my cell phone off in case Mike called and needed me, and the phone rang as I was interviewing this couple. It was Mike, calling to tell me that he felt better than he had in months.

"They drained off about a quart of fluid from my abdomen," he said. "I had a good breakfast and I feel great!"

In the back of my mind, I recalled that fluid in the abdomen is a sign of end-stage cancer. But it also could be lymphedema, an excess of fluid most often found in the arms of women who have had breast cancer surgery.

I went back to the interview, apologized for the interruption, and explained why I'd had to take the call.

"Sounds like he needs chocolate," the man said, handing me a small box.

That afternoon, I called Shannon and told her about the fluid on Mike's abdomen.

"It could be lymphedema," she said. "Let's just believe that for now."

I tried to put it out of my mind, but it was difficult. I would see Mike in a week and a half, and I could put my mind to rest then. I tried to convince myself that he would have put on a little weight and would have some color in his cheeks. After all, his scans were coming back clear, so that would have to mean there was no recurrence.

On the twenty-fifth, Mike had another doctor's appointment to discuss the results of the tests from the fluid that was drained from his abdomen. The fluid had been pretty clear, so we hoped that meant there would be no cancer cells.

I was on my way into work just before 10:00 a.m., when my cell phone rang. It was Mike.

"Mom, the cancer's back," he said. "They found it in the fluid. They can't cure it."

The doctor had told Mike he might have six months to a year, depending on how long the chemo treatments might keep it at bay.

"I hope I have enough time to travel to New York and say good-bye to people there," he said.

I could hardly hear his words, though. His first words were still swirling all about me, as though I were swimming —or drowning—in them.

How could this be? He was being treated at Duke, one of the best cancer care centers in the country. His doctors actually cared about him. And what about all the scans that came back negative? Why hadn't anyone seen the cancer if it was back?

"I'll be there this afternoon," I said.

Bob Gabordi had left the paper and transferred to another site within Gannett. His replacement, Susan Ihne, was out on medical leave. The acting executive editor's name was Phil, a somewhat reserved man who went by the book. I wasn't sure how he would react or whether he would even be willing to give me time off to deal with all of this.

I didn't speak to anyone. Rob would arrive at work in a few minutes and I was afraid of what might happen if I opened my mouth to say anything.

My fear was well founded. When Rob arrived and I went over to tell him, I fell apart. I didn't want to create a scene, but I couldn't hold it together. I sobbed as I choked out the words, "I just heard from Mike. The cancer's back. There's nothing they can do . . . I'm driving out there."

Rob went to tell Phil that we both would be out for the rest of the week as our colleagues gathered around me and held me up. Phil never came out of his office.

It was late afternoon by the time we got to Cary. I almost fell apart again when I saw Mike. He looked as frail as he had when he was in Savannah. His cheeks were sunken and dark circles surrounded his eyes. Janet was there already, and James had come home from work.

There was no room for us to stay in the apartment, so Rob and I took a room at a nearby motel.

After we checked in, I went across the street to an electronics store to walk around. I looked at photo printers, wondering whether I could figure out how to hook one up. I started to think that Mike would know and then it occurred to me that Mike wouldn't be here this time next year. I almost fell down in the store. My heart started racing and I couldn't catch my breath.

I managed to make it back to the motel room. Almost immediately, my phone rang. It was John Boyle.

"Phil wants a weather story," John joked. Phil was known for an obsession with weather and gas prices. "He wants twenty (column) inches, with a full analysis on how it might affect gas prices, which we'll cut to a brief and run on top of page B1. Oh, and he's docking you because you left early."

John could still make me laugh. Since a cold front was moving in, someone had gotten stuck with a weather story. I was glad it wasn't me, although I would research and file stories from Raleigh several times during the next few weeks.

The temperature dropped into the forties, and I hadn't brought a jacket with me, so we went to Target and I bought a red zip-front hoodie. As we were leaving the store, my eye caught sight of a woman holding a baby. She rocked gently back and forth as he fussed.

I wondered whether she knew how precious that child was and I had to resist the urge to plead with her to understand because that child might be taken from her.

"You just don't know," I wanted to say. "I used to be like you. I thought my child would outlive me and now I know he won't."

Back at the hotel room, I sat quietly, pretending to watch TV. Nothing was right. Nothing would ever be right again.

My phone rang again. It was another reporter asking if I could suggest some people to call on a news story about a homeless man who had died.

Tommy McMahan, a homeless man, had gone to the hospital emergency room with chest congestion. The doctor confirmed that he had pneumonia, gave him some antibiotics, and released him. Tommy argued that he wasn't well enough to spend the night outside, so someone called the police to take Tommy to jail, where he at least would be warm.

Tommy died in his cell that night.

I wondered whether Tommy would have been admitted to the hospital if he'd had insurance or money, and I couldn't help believing that he had died because he was poor and uninsured. I wondered if he had family who would mourn his death or whether he was alone.

I knew Mike would be surrounded by people who loved him when he died.

It didn't help.

Chapter 23

Before chemo would begin again, Mike had an appointment to see whether he was a candidate for a feeding tube that might help more nutrition get absorbed into his body. At this point, we were looking for anything that might kick-start even a short-term battle for more time.

Back when I was working for the nursing journal and reading studies that promised a longer survival rate of weeks or months, I was skeptical. What good is another month? Now I knew the answer. Anything that would buy us more time was worth considering—as long as it was quality time and not time spent in pain.

I wanted more time with my child. I wasn't ready to let go. I never would be.

"I guess whatever I was put here to do, I've done it," Mike said as we sat waiting for the gastroenterologist.

"That's not necessarily true," I said, even though I knew it was. He had finally turned over his home group's phone help line to someone else. There would be no more middle-of-the-night sessions to help someone work the steps.

A number of Mike's friends told me of knocking on his door in the wee hours of the morning and being invited in to talk. It didn't matter if he had worked until midnight and had an 8:00 a.m. class, Mike was willing to listen and to help.

"I never knew anybody as smart as Mike," James said. "He just knew the damnedest stuff."

"He made me a better person," his friend, Christian, said. "I always wanted to just go for coffee in the morning, but Mike insisted we do something nice for someone before coffee."

Christian was an Army veteran who wound up in bed with an underage girl after a night of drinking. It cost him dearly in Georgia, a state where someone convicted of statutory rape is placed in the same category as a man who rapes babies in a day care center. He was sentenced to a long probation and had to be registered as a sex offender. Mike helped him deal with the ramifications, including the difficulty of finding a place to live that wasn't within one thousand feet of a school, church, or park.

While we were visiting, Mike sat me and Rob down to talk about his living will.

"I want you to know I'm going to ask Shannon to be my health care power of attorney," Mike said. "I know you'd follow my wishes, but I don't want you to have to make the decision to let me go."

I would have followed his wishes, but I felt a sense of relief. It wasn't likely there would be any decisions to make. When the time came, Mike would come home with me and Rob and we would care for him until the end came. There would be no CPR, no call to 9-1-1.

#

At the end of the week, as Rob and I were getting ready to go home, we got a call from Mike. The tubes in his back were leaking and he needed to go to the emergency room.

Because of his illness, the nurses put him in a private room to avoid exposure to pathogens. We waited. Noon came and went, then one, then two. Mike sent us out to get some lunch. TGI Friday's was right around the corner, and although Rob and I don't usually eat at chain restaurants, it was quick. We told the waitress we were in a rush and we were in and out in about twenty minutes.

It was three o'clock before Mike finally went in for the minor surgery to replace the tubes to his kidneys. It should be done every few months, the doctor said.

While he was gone, I took a look at his chart and read the words, "adult male with metastatic colon cancer." I knew the description was accurate, but there was so much more to my son than that sentence. There was his passion for music and good food, his love of philosophy, his compassion for others, his wicked sense of humor.

But it all seemed to have been boiled down to "adult male with metastatic colon cancer." That was all we had left, it appeared.

Mike would have to wait a couple more hours to go home, just to be sure there were no complications, so Janet arrived and sat with him and we left to go back to Asheville.

The new tubes likely would leak as well because he had no body fat left. Once Mike was home, James would devise a solution using menstrual pads and cloth tape that kept Mike comfortable.

I would be back the following Monday to take him to his first chemo appointment.

I went back to work six days after finding out Mike was dying. Bruce Steele, my direct supervisor, put me on light duty, knowing I wasn't capable of doing anything too complex. My colleagues all let me know they were there for me and Rob—all except for Phil, who continued to avoid me.

Finally, on Thursday, Phil literally bumped into me outside his office.

"I've been meaning to tell you I'm sorry about your son," he said. "I just didn't know what to say."

"I'm sorry about your son would have been fine," I said. "I don't care if you're uncomfortable with it. In fact, you should be uncomfortable with it. But you need to say it."

Maybe I should have let him off the hook, but he was the boss, and it was important to me that a boss at least say he or she is sorry about the hell I was going through. I sat him down and explained how important it is for a boss to acknowledge what his or her employees were going through.

"I'm a pretty private person," he said.

"That's fine at home, but not when you're the boss at work," I said. "You want to be a leader; this is part of it."

Months later, I would make him go and speak to a reporter whose father had been diagnosed with terminal lung cancer.

\#

I needed to work while I was in Raleigh because for every day I didn't file a story I was charged with a vacation day. I didn't know what I would do when I ran out of vacation days.

I went back to Cary the following Monday so I could get Mike to chemo first thing. I hated the thought of infusions of poison being pushed into his body, but we all wanted a little more time with him. If the chemo could hold the cancer at bay, even for a few months, Mike thought it was worth it.

The nurse put him in a private room for the chemo, since it was his first infusion of the new cocktail.

He sat on the bed. "I so don't want to be here."

"You don't have to do this," I heard myself say. I wanted to yell at myself. What the hell was I doing telling him it was OK to let go whenever he was ready? What about if I wasn't ready?

"No, I want to try," he said.

The nurse took me aside and took my hand. "You'll know when it's time to let go," she said. "That's not to say you'll want to, but you'll know."

First he received a powerful antihistamine to combat the reaction they knew his body would have. Within a few minutes he vomited anyway. They gave him more antihistamine and he drifted off to sleep.

The nurse told me he likely would sleep for the rest of his infusion if I wanted to go for a walk or get something to eat. I wandered out to the waiting room, where there was food for family members, and had a bite to eat, sat down and worked on a jigsaw puzzle, and then went back into the room.

I had my laptop with me, but I could only stare at the screen. Today would have to be a vacation day. How was I supposed to concentrate on anything when my son was getting chemotherapy? How would I ever be able to concentrate on anything again? And why couldn't I find someone to talk to who had been through this nightmare? How was I supposed to feel, and what was I supposed to do? I felt as though I must be the first person to ever be in this situation.

After I got Mike home, I went out and bought all the foods I thought he might eat—just as James had been doing for months. Naturally, I included several Cadbury Crème Eggs. The main thing now was getting calories into him.

The next day, I interviewed people from the NC Division of Mental Health, Developmental Disabilities and Substance Abuse Services about changes being made to the system that might make it easier for people to get treatment.

#

I had heard reports of people being released from psychiatric hospitals with no discharge plans or with nowhere safe to go. The state had reduced the number of beds available in its hospitals, with the reasoning that "reform" would allow people to live and seek treatment in their home communities.

But treatment options weren't popping up as had been planned. Medicaid rates were low and many private practitioners couldn't afford to take Medicaid patients and still stay in business.

Psychiatric hospitals were operating at 110 to 120 percent of capacity and local hospitals were overwhelmed. Many of the people who needed hospitalization were landing in jail. It was estimated that two-thirds of the people in the state's jails had mental health or substance abuse problems—or both.

In some of the smaller towns, police officers who responded to crises had to transport patients to the closest psychiatric hospital, which might be two or more hours away. The person had to be turned down by two facilities before the state hospital could accept him or her, and the police officer had to stay with the person, and then go file a report. It was costing more in overtime than some of these small towns could afford—in addition to leaving gaps in the patrol coverage at home as an officer had to drive two or more hours each way.

State Senator Martin Nesbitt, who was in charge of the legislative oversight committee, was looking for answers to why things were in such disarray. But the entire Department of Health and Human Services was in disarray. As things went wrong, Secretary Carmen Hooker Odom was trying to correct them, but it meant policy changes almost every week.

The system wasn't getting a chance to settle down and perform because the initial changes had happened too fast, and too many people had fallen through the cracks as the nonprofit service providers went out of business. The Department tried to increase oversight of the agencies that were left, but that just meant agency employees were spending the bulk of their time preparing for and conducting audits.

There was plenty for me to do in Raleigh, so it appeared that only actual chemo days would become vacation days.

I went home late Wednesday afternoon and Danny and Hazen arrived in town to visit Mike. Danny said Mike looked pretty depressed, but Hazen still believed Mike would somehow pull through.

Chapter 24

Mike's next chemo was scheduled two weeks after his first. He still hadn't gained any weight.

"You need to gain two pounds before your next treatment," the physician assistant told Mike as we headed into the chemo room.

This time we were in the main room, in one of several rows of recliners. An older couple was next to us—the man was reading a book by one of the right-wing TV pundits. We nodded at each other and I hoped he wouldn't want to start a conversation. I didn't have the fortitude to endure a glowing review of the ideas of Rush Limbaugh, Ann Coulter, Glenn Beck, or Bill O'Reilly.

Fortunately, they kept to themselves.

After Mike drifted off, I went for a walk outside and wound up on the steps of the Duke Chapel, which actually looks more like a cathedral. I went inside and found a quiet spot downstairs out of the main sanctuary.

"Please, God," I prayed. "Just two pounds."

I repeated it again and again.

I knew we had limited time left, but I hoped the chemo would do some good, perhaps hold the cancer at bay for a few months.

James and I continued to try and feed him, and he was eating a little food several times a day. He still loved fresh bagels (he could eat about a half of one), Frosted Flakes with chocolate soy milk, coffee, French toast with butter (no syrup), and chocolate.

It wouldn't be enough.

Before his next appointment, on March 18, Mike sat down on the couch in his living room and said, "I'm ready for this to be over."

Still, when we went in for his appointment and he stepped on the scale, he had lost another pound.

He turned to me with a look of utter surprise. "I tried!" he said.

"I know," I replied.

#

There was nothing more to say. Chemo wasn't working, and his time was even more limited than we had thought.

Dr. Hurwitz came in to talk to Mike, his eyes filling with tears. "You're a good person, Mike," he said. "You don't deserve this."

He hugged us both and again told us how sorry he was that more couldn't be done.

It was good to have a doctor who cared, after hearing Dr. Hammen in Savannah dismissively tell Mike there was nothing more he could do. Herb Hurwitz had given us two more years with Mike, most of it pretty good quality. He had fought alongside us instead of giving up and walking away. He had kept us informed about everything instead of keeping knowledge of any life-threatening conditions to himself. I honestly believed everything that could be done had been tried.

He recommended Mike go home to Asheville with me.

"Can I wait until the weekend?" Mike asked.

"You should go today," he said. "You want to enjoy what time you have. I don't know how long that will be, but you deserve to enjoy it."

As we were leaving the clinic, I grabbed a wheelchair for Mike so he wouldn't have to walk to the parking garage.

"How much time do you think I have?" Mike asked me. "Maybe two weeks?"

"I hope more than that," I said.

I was trying not to think about life without Mike. I couldn't imagine it when I did think about it. So I kept telling myself, "He's here now, so I have to appreciate that."

I think this is when I began to tell myself that my heart would stop when his did, that I wouldn't have to go on after he died. I would go with him instead of having to go on without him.

When we got back to the apartment, James confided in me.

"I'm so scared," he said. "I'm afraid I'll come home from work and find him dead. I don't think I could handle that."

James had cared for Mike for a year now, changing dressings, cooking, listening, running errands, and paying bills. I didn't want him to come home and discover Mike had died alone during the day.

"He's coming home with me today," I said. "You can come too if you want."

I had to call Hazen and tell him there would be no more treatment.

"But there has to be something we can do!" he said. "How about a medical trial? There has to be something."

He was sobbing and I was getting angry. Where was all his compassion the whole time Mike had been sick? And why did he wait so long to recognize Mike hadn't received what he needed?

"You know what you can do?" I snapped. "You can send money. The kid has lived in abject poverty for three years while he waited for his disability to be approved. We've all helped him; maybe you can step up."

I knew he could afford it, and I was angry that he hadn't given Mike any money before. Mike hadn't asked, and we all had joked for years about how cheap Hazen was. But this was inexcusable in my mind at this moment. He could have asked Mike at any time whether he needed anything. In reality, Mike likely would have told him everything was OK, but when he would try to tell me that, I knew better, so why couldn't his father?

We received a letter a few days earlier saying Mike's disability had finally been approved—thirty-six months after he first applied. His first check should arrive in a couple of weeks.

"I never thought he'd die from this," Hazen sobbed. I didn't want to be angry, but I couldn't help it. "I figured if I could survive it, he could. I didn't know his disability hasn't started."

"You never asked," I said. His own disability had been approved in a matter of weeks because his company had helped him get it. He'd had the best health care, the best disability attorney that money could buy. As soon as he was diagnosed, he was treated.

Mike was rejected, neglected, and kicked to the curb. His gastroenterologist had first refused to perform the screening tests—despite Mike's medical need—then had found a blockage and ignored it. His oncologists had let him nearly starve to death after radiation caused a stricture in his small intestine. Then his gastroenterologist failed to treat a life-threatening infection in the incision.

Rather than argue with Hazen, I told him I had to help Mike pack and hung up. I didn't want to talk about his money and privilege because he wouldn't understand.

We called Janet at work and she came right over. Together the four of us packed the few belongings Mike would need, including what I called his super-jet-turbo computer—the one he built specifically for gaming. It was one of a dozen or more computers that he and James had built together. Most had been given to people who were newly sober.

We packed all of Mike's plaid pajama pants and T-shirts, which was all he had worn for months, a few books, the video game console, and some games. By two o'clock we were on the road to Asheville.

An hour into the drive, Mike was shifting uncomfortably in his seat.

"Are you taking your pain pills?" I asked.

He was, but his backside, which had no fat, was uncomfortable. We stopped at J&R Outlet to get a memory foam pillow and laughed about his sorry ass.

He was calm now. He knew what was coming, but he also knew it was inevitable, and he had stopped fighting. He was more his old self than he had been in months.

When we got home, I helped him up the front steps and deposited him on the couch. He was going to be in the guest room, but he wanted to sit in the living room for awhile first.

I called hospice and they said they would be there the next morning.

James and Janet arrived that night and we went shopping for some of the things we would need, including a walkie-talkie so we could take turns being on Mike duty. James was allergic to the cats, so after spending one night in the house, he took a motel room.

The hospice nurse arrived in the morning and asked what we needed. We didn't even know. She arranged for a hospital bed, a tray table, a walker, and other supplies, all of which arrived that afternoon.

During the medical history, the nurse asked Mike whether he used tobacco.

"Yes, and I'm not about to quit," he said.

She looked at him for a moment and asked whether he used drugs or alcohol.

"I did," he said, "but I sobered up eleven years ago."

"And what was your drug of choice?"

I could see his eyes light up. "Whaddaya got?"

"Excuse me?"

"I was what you call a garbage head," he said, obviously pleased at her shocked reaction. "If it would alter my consciousness, I'd do it."

#

The social worker and the hospice doctor would come the next day, but we were happy to have Mike set up in a hospital bed in the guest room.

After he was all settled in, Mike sat me down "You know, I think I'm going to give up the Cancer Card," he said.

I had to catch my breath. I hadn't expected this.

"I have a better card now," he said, starting to smile. "It's the I'm Dying Card. Get me some coffee, OK? I'm dying."

I made a pot of coffee and brought him a cup with plenty of soy milk and sugar.

"By the way," he said. "You're about to get a card that's pretty much untrumpable. It's the Dead Kid Card."

"I don't want it," I said.

"Doesn't matter," he said. "You'll have it, and I want you to use it in a positive way, OK? Don't sue anybody, even though they deserve it. You don't want that kind of negativity in your life."

I told him I wanted to advocate for universal access to health care and he gave me his blessing. Three years ago he hadn't believed people deserved government-paid care, but his own situation taught him that everyone deserves care as a basic human right.

I didn't believe I'd actually do advocacy work, though, because I still thought I'd be going with him.

Chapter 25

On Thursday, the social worker and the doctor came.

Hazen and Scott showed up too. It was hard to get Hazen into the house because it's on a hill and the only way to get to the main level is by stairs.

Scott helped his dad get up the stairs to the back deck.

While the doctor was in with Mike, Hazen chatted with the social worker. I went about doing housework and prepping for dinner. We were going to have a lot of people to feed over the coming days as Mike's friends and family members came to say good-bye. Friends were stopping by with food, but it felt good to be in the kitchen.

As I was working, I heard Hazen telling a story I hadn't heard in years. He was playing basketball in a staff-student game in college, and being the klutz that he was, he made a layup shot and his hand caught the net. He came down flat on his back.

"You could hear everyone in the room gasp," he said. "There was no other sound until I jumped up and threw my hands in the air. Then everybody cheered and cheered."

It was, word for word, the same way he had told it to me more than thirty years earlier.

Hazen and Scott went in to see Mike after the doctor came out.

I took that opportunity to ask the doctor how much longer we might have with Mike.

"I think we have to measure his life in days or weeks now instead of months," the doctor said. "His body isn't absorbing nutrients anymore. But he's comfortable and in good spirits. That means a lot."

When the social worker went in to talk to Mike, I looked out and saw Scott in the front yard, sobbing. I went out to talk to him.

"This is really hard," I said. "We so want to change it and we can't. It's OK for us to feel terrible about it."

A half hour later, the social worker came out. "In all my time doing this, I've never met anyone like him," she said. "He's so centered, so wise. He's remarkable."

I knew that already.

Friday was Good Friday and Shannon and the kids arrived from Fayetteville. They would spend Easter with us, although she insisted on staying in a motel instead of at the house.

"You have enough going on," she said.

#

Someone at the office left on my desk a large plastic container with coins. It came to about $200. It didn't take me long to figure out who it was—Dave Russell, a quirky, creative, rather twisted man who identified with Mike's jackass nature.

"Tell him he can't pay bills with it," Dave said. "He has to buy something fun."

Mike thought about it for awhile and decided he wanted a couple of video games. I deposited the coins in his bank account and he shopped online.

He made his choices and was about to hit "submit," when he paused.

"Wait, wait," he said, going back to a previous screen. "Next day delivery. I might not have five to seven business days and I want to be the first one to play with these."

For a moment, everyone in the room was horrified, but then he began to laugh.

"So glad I remembered that," he said.

That afternoon, James and Janet decided to get out of the house and look for a wheelchair for Mike. It would be dubbed "the Mike-around." We would be able to take him out on the deck when the weather was nice.

"You know hospice would have brought a wheelchair," I said.

They knew, but they wanted it to come from them.

The next errand was to buy stickers so we could pimp his ride. We pimped the walker too.

Friday night would bring a carload of people from Savannah, mostly friends from his home group. The house was filled with laughter as everyone told Mike stories. He loved hearing about what a jackass he had been.

The visits were exhausting for him, but he enjoyed them nevertheless.

Danny and Jennifer and the kids came, too, and Mike spoke with each of them, one-on-one.

Lauren asked whether he was "saved." He told her he was and gave her his sobriety date.

He told them how much he loved each of them and asked them to remember him as the silly person he was before he got sick.

He asked Trey whether he understood what was happening.

"I do," Trey said. "You're going to Heaven soon."

Danny had a hard time sitting with Mike.

"It's just so hard to see him like that," he told me.

"Don't see him as a dying person," I said. "See him as Mike because that's still who he is."

During the week, I was trying to put in an appearance at work every day so I could be paid. The day after Easter, I went in.

"You know, you don't need to be here," John Boyle told me. "You don't get a do-over on this. Spend your time with Mike."

I couldn't afford to run out of vacation time, though.

So John and others came up with a solution. One by one they went to Human Resources and donated some of their vacation days to Rob and me. More than thirty days were donated before the publisher, Randy Hammer, heard about it. He hadn't known Rob and I were being charged vacation days as we cared for Mike.

I don't know what Randy said to Phil, but after they spoke, Randy came out to the newsroom and told the staff they could have their vacation days back and that the company would pay Rob and me for whatever time we needed.

"He had tears in his eyes," John told me.

I went in the next day to thank Randy, and he told me he was still praying for a miracle. I told him it would be better to pray for strength for Rob and me because there wasn't going to be a miracle. He seemed surprised that I could lose faith when I needed it most, but I told him I had to face reality, and the reality was that my son would die in the coming days.

I didn't want to ask him to stop trying to give me false hope, but when someone's loved one is dying and you tell them you're hoping for a miracle, that's what you're doing. You're telling them that if they pray and hope hard enough, the person will recover, and if you don't, they'll die.

I stopped by the desk of my friend Dale and asked whether he could bring Mike a twelve-step meeting on Wednesday. I knew he would appreciate it, even though he and his Savannah friends had held a meeting over the weekend.

James and Janet were at the house every day, helping to cook and clean, looking after Mike's needs. James was still the only one Mike would allow to change his dressings.

Janet's mother came, as did my niece, Christina.

"Grams sent you this," Christina said as she pulled a cross-eyed stuffed bear out of her bag. "It's Idiot Bear."

We put it on the bed next to the football-shaped tangle of yarn that was "boo bankie."

As did everyone else, Christina brought Cadbury Crème Eggs. By now there were dozens of them on the dresser.

Janet and I offered him one, but he shook his head.

"Believe it or not, I've had enough for this year," he said. "Maybe next . . . maybe somebody else would like them."

When Dale and the others arrived for the meeting, I had baked cookies and made coffee. By now, Mike was allowed to smoke in the house, and James could smoke with him if he wanted. I don't think anyone smoked at that meeting, though.

As they were leaving, I thanked Dale for bringing the meeting to Mike.

"No," he said, "I have to thank you. It was a remarkable meeting. Thank you for the privilege of letting me get to know Mike."

The weekend brought more people, this time from Raleigh and Cary. Christian was still hoping to get permission from his probation officer to come say good-bye to Mike. He didn't make it, but they did speak several times.

On Saturday, I counted sixteen people in the house and yard. It was exhausting for me, and for Mike, who threw everyone out of the room when he needed to nap. Only James was allowed to stay, and when I peeked in, I saw Mike asleep in the bed and James snoozing in the chair.

By Sunday afternoon, most of the crowd had left, Mike was asleep and my friends, Kristy, Kathleen, and I were just climbing out of the hot tub when the doorbell rang.

It was a woman from the neighborhood, furious that cars were parked along the side of her road. I had never met her before and I was not pleased with her tone. I let her rant for a few moments before speaking.

"These people are here to say good-bye to my son," I said quietly. "He'll be dead in a few days and then you can have your road back."

I started to close the door.

"Wait! I'm sorry. I didn't know. Is there anything I can do?"

I told her she could remember this before she started screaming at a neighbor again, and she could drive carefully, then I closed the door.

When Mike heard about it, he thought it was hilarious. People who are mean before they know what's going on deserve to be shocked, he said. It served her right.

A week later, another neighbor would stop by to say she had seen all the cars and prayed that we would be OK, whatever was going on.

Chapter 26

By Sunday night, everyone had left. Even James and Janet had gone back to Raleigh to pick up mail and get more time off work.

Mike and I sat in his room. I crocheted while he slept, and we watched TV and chatted when he was awake.

"You know, Mom, I can go to a hospice facility if you want some respite," he said.

"No way," I said. "I'm taking care of you. I have enough help. I want you here—that is, if you want to be here."

"Yeah, I'm good."

I stayed home on Monday and Rob went to work. Mike and I decided to watch a *Star Trek* marathon and nibble on dark chocolate.

We were watching the *Deep Space Nine* episode where the Klingon officer Worf joins the crew of the station. We had watched an original series episode, a *Next Generation* episode, and now this one.

"You know, Mom, I'm having a good time here," Mike said.

I looked at him, weighing less than one hundred pounds, unable to eat more than a nibble or two, starting to develop skin sores. His body had betrayed him in a dozen different ways and his pain was barely managed.

"Really?"

"Well, yeah. Look at me. I have everything I need: my TV, my video games, dark chocolate, pee bucket (a blue bucket where we could empty his pee bags without getting him out of bed), my cigarettes, *Star Trek*, Boo Bankie, Idiot Bear, and you, my personal valet."

He meant it. He had been able to find joy even in this circumstance—confined to a hospital bed in a small room. He was living his life to the limit, even when it was so severely limited.

His arm was developing a bedsore, so I asked if I could wrap it in a super soft cloth that I had found at the craft store when we were looking for stickers. He started to tell me he would be OK, but I picked up his arm and wrapped it anyway.

"Wow, that does feel better," he said.

His arm was so thin I felt as though I could break it just by picking it up. It weighed nothing. I knew I could scoop him out of the bed with little effort. Time was getting short.

The next morning, I went in to see Mike before running to the office for a few minutes.

"I'm feeling pretty weak today," he said as he lit a cigarette. "I think I'll just stay in bed."

I had bought him a carton of cigarettes the day before. If having a cigarette made him feel better, then he could have as many as he wanted. The no-smoking-in-the-house rule was gone as long as he was with us.

I spent an hour at the office, ran a couple of errands, and then went home about noon. Mike was napping so I had lunch. The hospice nurse was coming in a little while, so I decided to let him sleep until she arrived.

At about one-thirty, the nurse and I went in to see how he was doing, and I couldn't rouse him.

She had a little more luck, but he was distant, foggy in his responses.

"He's between here and there," she told me.

He was in the process of dying and it could be a day or longer, she said. I knew he would go quickly.

I called James and Janet, then Danny.

"I don't think you'll have time to get here," I said. "I just wanted you to know."

I pulled my chair up next to the bed and took his hand. He opened his eyes and tried to tell me he loved me, but all he could get out was, "I lo—I lo—"

"I love you, too," I said. He smiled and closed his eyes again.

"You'll want to take care of yourself," the nurse said as Rob came into the room. "He could hover between here and there for hours, or even days."

"No, he's going," I said. "I know my son, and if he's decided it's time to go, he'll go quickly."

My other argument was that I brought him into this world and I would see him out.

I continued to hold his hand and talk to him as Rob went downstairs to e-mail work and tell them he wouldn't be in.

A little after three-thirty, he opened his eyes again and reached out with his free hand.

"Ellen," he whispered.

Shannon and I had talked about Ellen coming to fetch him home.

"She's so bossy," I said to her.

"I can hear her," Shannon said. *"He's my nephew, dammit, I'll go get him!"*

And here she was, even though Mike was the only one who could see her.

\#

It was time for him to go.

At just after 3:45 p.m., he stopped breathing.

"He's gone," the nurse said.

I sat there for a moment, stunned that I was still breathing. I was supposed to go with him. I wasn't supposed to be here without him. It wasn't right. Maybe it would take a little while for me to join him.

I seemed calm, but I was in a panic. Why was I still here? What the hell was I supposed to do now that he was gone?

I leaned over and kissed his face. "I'm so grateful I got to be your mom," I said, and I went to the top of the stairs.

"Rob, he's gone," I said.

Rob bounded up the stairs and into the room, sobbing.

"Oh, Mikey, Mikey," he cried as he reached the bed.

The phone rang. It was Scott, wanting to know if there was time for him and his dad to make it.

"No, he just died," I said. "But if you and your dad and mom want to come and be with the family, you're welcome to be here."

A minute later, the phone rang again. It was Danny, sobbing.

"He's gone?"

"Just a couple of minutes ago, yes."

The line in our lives had been drawn. There was *before Mike died* and there was *now*. Everything would be defined by this. Mike was here; Mike was gone.

And I was still here.

Damn.

I called John Boyle and asked him to let people in the newsroom know that Mike had died.

"I don't know what to say," he said. "I'll let everyone know, and let me know if there's anything more I can do."

Five minutes later, he called back.

"I don't want to seem inappropriate, but do you know what today is?" he asked.

"Oh my God, it's April first," I gasped. "He left on April Fool's Day! No wonder he was in such a hurry."

Within twenty minutes, the hospice chaplain, Reverend Buddy Corbin, arrived. I had met Buddy when I was covering religion at the paper. When he heard that my son was dying, he called and asked what he could do. We went to lunch and talked about Mike and about my feelings about his impending death. When the nurse called to report Mike's death, Buddy came right away.

"Would you like me to pray him out?" he asked.

We nodded. I don't remember what he said. I only remember the sound of my own heartbeat, persistent, strong.

Damn.

The nurse had gotten rid of Mike's pain meds and called the funeral home. Mike would be cremated. There would be no "viewing." Mike wanted all of us to remember him in life.

As we stood in the room with Buddy and the nurse, Rob looked at Mike.

"He could be such a pain in the ass," Rob said. Buddy and the nurse stared at him and the nurse started to speak.

"No, no, he could be," I said. "It was a point of pride for him that he could annoy people, especially people who were annoying to him."

We had called our pastor, Joe Hoffman, who arrived a few minutes after Buddy finished praying. Moments later, the funeral home folks arrived. I kissed Michael good-bye and went into the kitchen.

I didn't want to see my child taken out in a body bag.

When they had the gurney in the living room, the woman called me to come and sign some papers and I asked her to come into the kitchen. She repeated that she just wanted me to sign some papers, and Joe asked her to walk into the kitchen.

"She would rather avoid seeing her child in a body bag," Joe said. "Please just step into the kitchen."

I wondered how someone who worked for a funeral home could be so insensitive. This was business to her, but not to me. I had just lost my child, and she wanted me to lean the clipboard on his lifeless body and sign my name.

When they were gone, I came into the living room and we each poured a glass of wine to toast Mike and his legacy of laughter, wisdom, and strength.

Shannon called as we were sitting. She had been out of service range and saw a missed call from me.

"Auntie, they threw me a rainbow!" she said. "I was in the mall and I came out, noticed your number, and there was this beautiful rainbow right in front of me."

#

I sat outside for a few minutes after everything had calmed down. A neighbor saw me and walked up the driveway.

"Mike died about an hour and a half ago," I said. My voice still sounded strangely calm to me. "I'm not sure what's next. I guess we have to arrange a funeral."

Mike had made several requests. He wanted me to read 23rd Psalm. He wanted "Tears in Heaven," "Amazing Grace," and "Et Tout Le Monde" played. He wanted James to speak because he knew James would know what to say.

James and Janet arrived at about seven and we decided to go out to eat. We wound up at Applebee's, mainly because it's the closest non-fast-food restaurant to the house.

As we waited for our food, Rob turned to me.

"Nobody ever loved anybody more than you loved Mike," he said.

"It didn't do him much good in the end," I said.

We all loved him fiercely, but it hadn't saved his life in the face of a broken health care system. We hadn't been able to get Dr. Hammen to care, or the oncologists who took a wait-and-see attitude and nearly allowed him to starve to death from a stricture in his small intestine, and then his incision had been allowed to fester. By the time we found Dr. Hurwitz, it was too late to save Mike's life.

I knew the health care system as well as anyone. I had written about people who were not able to get the help they needed, and some had been able to get care as a result. But I hadn't been able to save my own son.

In the final weeks of Mike's life, I had written about a three-year-old boy with leukemia whose insurance company called his last hope of remission "experimental," even though the physicians disagreed. His father was a firefighter who put his life on the line all the time, and his child was going to die without one last attempt to save his life.

I wrote the story and the insurance company changed its mind. He got the treatment, but it was too late to save him. He died the same week Mike did.

He saw angels coming for him before he died, his mother told me. I told her about my sister coming to fetch Mike home.

We knew they were safe, but it was of little comfort.

Chapter 27

Danny arrived late that night. The next day, a steady stream of people stopped by. By mid-afternoon, fifteen women were in the house, most of them from Piecemakers, the group of women from church that met once a week to work on our own projects and joint projects.

A few weeks earlier, just after we got word that Mike was dying, we had all met and had Communion together. We didn't have wine available, so we used gin and tonics—but the important thing was that we were together.

Val Collins, who was executive director of the local women's shelter, stopped by and I gave her Mike's video game console. Most of the games weren't appropriate for children, but a few were, and she took them gratefully.

My friends cooked and cleaned, laughed and cried with me, hugged me and listened to us tell stories about Mike.

Later, after most people had left, Danny started telling stories of the things he and Mike had done while they were at their father's house during the summer.

"We found a briefcase one time and we thought it made us look really official," Danny said. "So we took it and went door-to-door telling people we were collecting money for our church youth mission trip to Guatemala."

"Guatemala?"

"We thought it sounded good, and it must have because people gave us money. We made a couple hundred dollars over the course of the summer."

I was torn between feeling ashamed that my kids were con men and being proud of their cleverness.

"What did you do with the money?"

"We bought soda and snacks and shared it with all the kids at the Boys' Club."

Most of the kids at the Boys' Club were low-income. Danny and Michael's dad paid full price for day care services, so they could get away with a lot. No one asked where the goodies came from, Danny said.

They also convinced kids that a house in the neighborhood was haunted and charged them admission to go in and experience the ghost (Mike making noises and throwing things).

"You didn't do this kind of stuff at home, did you?" I asked.

"You weren't as gullible as Dad," he said.

\#

Susan Ihne, who had been out on medical leave, was back in the newsroom. She brought in a cooler, which everyone would fill up with food, bring it to us in the evening, and then would take the cooler back to fill up again the next day. It was a lot of food, but we had a lot of company and it was good to be able to offer people something to eat.

Doug Maher, a newsroom colleague who grew up in on the Gulf Coast in Mississippi, brought red beans and rice. It was a huge pot of food, but it only lasted a day or so.

Kristy Carter came by to help us figure out what music and photos we wanted for a slide show during the memorial service, which we decided should be in Savannah. A minister there was in Mike's home group and called to ask if she could officiate.

Elliott, one of the people Mike sponsored, now a chef, said the home group would provide all the food we needed for the reception after the service.

We reserved several rooms at a nearby motel for family and friends from Raleigh, Asheville, and New England. Christina would fly into Savannah with my mother and would tend to her during the trip.

At home, we were getting food from people at church as well as from the newsroom. People stopped by with food, beer and wine, and one of the photographers, John Coutlakis, gave me a bottle of eighteen-year-old single-malt Scotch.

I tried to tell him the gift was just too much, but he waved me off.

"I'm forty-two years old and I live with my mother," he said. "I can afford it."

Janet and I designed the brochure that would be given out at the memorial service with photos of Mike, the order of service, and my eulogy. The planning kept us busy.

Robin called to say she would arrive in Asheville on Tuesday after the memorial service because she thought I would need her there more after everyone else had left.

Before leaving for the memorial service, I stopped in at the county Register of Deeds office to pick up Mike's death certificate. James told me the cable company wanted to see it before they'd change the service over to his name.

"They want an original," James had said.

"They get a copy unless they want to pay ten dollars for an original. Tell them to call me if they have a problem with that," I said.

But the death certificate wasn't ready. I was told to try back the following week. I still had to close his checking account and take care of other paperwork, but it could wait.

\#

After my father died, Mike said he wanted the same kind of memorial service. He wanted people to laugh and remember his jokes, not grieve his passing.

We brought his leather jacket, his New York Yankees baseball cap, and his picture to set atop the altar. I asked James to speak first and to tell the "bagging the barista" story to set the tone.

"I was an only child," he began, "so I never knew you could love someone more than you love yourself until Mike taught me how. Mike was my brother."

He was starting to choke up and I was afraid he wouldn't be able to finish, but he took a deep breath and continued.

"He was such a jackass!"

The entire church burst into laughter and applause and Mike's memorial service turned into a rather bizarre twelve-step meeting. Mike's spirit was in the room.

James told the story of how Mike saw his colostomy as "a sort of blessing," because once gas became trapped in the bag, it had to be released, and the stench could be overwhelming. Imagine a thousand farts.

"He would save it up," James said. "And if he was insulted, he would bag you."

Mike hated what he called corporate food, and he saw Starbucks as being in the same category as McDonald's. When he and James stopped at one to get coffee, the barista was, in James's words, "snotty as hell." Mike got his coffee and walked over to James, who was adding milk and sugar to his coffee.

"Get ready to run," he said. "I'm baggin' this place."

More than a few of the hundred or so people at the service had experienced "the bag."

As people got up to speak, they introduced themselves and were greeted with the twelve-step, "Hey . . ."

My eighty-three-year-old mother got up to speak. She struggled to get the microphone down to her four-foot, ten-inch level and started to speak.

"I'm Michael's grandmothuh," she started in her Massachusetts accent.

"HEY, MIKE'S GRAMDMA!"

Hazen got up ("HEY, MIKE'S DAD!") and told the story of Mike and Danny jumping off the roof into the pool. A neighbor called him at work to tell him what they had been doing, but he was really getting concerned because now Mike was struggling to get his bike up onto the roof. Hazen made it home in time to prevent any major injuries.

For more than an hour the stories continued, most of them funny, but some deeply moving. Mike had left in indelible impression on many, many lives.

"You always knew when Mike walked into a meeting, it would be a good meeting," one friend said. "He'd come in late, smelling of fryer oil and say something that would change your life."

Mike went to beginner meetings often because he knew he could help people there. Being new to recovery is difficult and Mike enjoyed easing the way for people.

"He pulled me out of the gutter," another friend said. "He saved my life."

When the minister spoke, she talked about Michael's dignity.

"As a recovering alcoholic, if you freeze to death in the gutter, but you're sober, you have died with dignity. Mike faced neglect, pain, and debilitation, and he maintained his sobriety. Mike died with dignity."

I thought about all the indignities he had suffered—being denied care, being told he should get financial counseling when what he needed was surgery, being ignored—and still, he stayed sober. Even when he knew he was dying and alcohol wouldn't have hastened his death, he stayed sober.

We decided to end the service on a bright note, and after asking everyone to remain seated for one final song, we played Eric Idle's classic "Always Look on the Bright Side of Life."

Mike loved Monty Python and had memorized most of their songs, including "Every Sperm is Sacred" and "The Philosopher's Song."

I wasn't sure if people would be offended or amused, but it only took a moment for people to realize what was playing and to begin clapping and singing along.

At the end of the service, Elliott's mother came over to hug me.

"It should have been my son who died," she said. "But your son saved his life. I just want you to know that."

Several other people told me stories of how they would have died without Mike's help. They could knock on his door any time of the day or night and he would answer. He was a great listener and he always had remarkable insight into whatever was troubling people.

He was a very old soul.

The home group put out a huge buffet that included pulled pork, side dishes, and a number of homemade desserts.

"Mike loved good food," Elliott told me. "He deserves the best we can do for his send-off."

#

Several of Mike's friends cornered me in the churchyard.

"We wanted you to know that we're going to celebrate Mike's life every year on April first," one young woman said. "Were going to call it Mike Day; we're going to wear plaid and we're going to go out of our way to do something silly."

He could ask for no greater honor, I told her. It was a brilliant idea, and we would celebrate the same way.

The next morning, we all met for breakfast at Denny's. As my mother got out of the car, she groaned and said, "Oh, don't get old." She did this often, and it had been getting on my nerves for a long time. This time, I reacted.

"Mother, I think Mike would have loved to get old," I said. "He thought of every day as a gift, no matter how much he suffered. Please, just stop saying that in front of me."

She hadn't thought about that, she said. She was just frustrated with how frail she was becoming. But she said she would try to stop thinking that way.

She never did enjoy life the way Mike did, although her sister, Marguerite—Auntie Re—always enjoyed whatever adventure each day brought.

When I was a teenager and my mother insisted this was the best time of my life, I wondered whether it was worth going on. Perhaps I should just end it there, rather than face even worse pain. But Auntie Re told me each year got better for her, and when she was in her late seventies, she told me how much she enjoyed getting old. Even with the physical limitations of aging, she said, there were adventures each day. Some days it was fun to sit on the front porch and watch the foxes catch mice in the meadow. Other days she and Uncle Ralph felt good enough to put the canoe in the water. There was joy always.

Chapter 28

After we got home from Savannah, Robin came for a few days. We spent a lot of time talking about Mike and about what I should do next. I planned on staying at the newspaper and writing about social justice issues, hoping that if people were educated about the issues, they might elect candidates who would do something about the woefully inadequate health care system.

I tried again to get Mike's death certificate, but it still wasn't ready.

Robin's visit ended and I became restless. I pulled out the old reel mower and began mowing our one-acre lot.

Back and forth.

Back and forth.

All my brain had to do was think about back and forth. It wasn't capable of doing any more than that. I couldn't read, nor could I sit still in front of the TV for any length of time. My mind was incapable of focusing on anything.

By late afternoon, I had mowed the entire yard—an acre—just in time for John Boyle and another colleague, Nancy Bompey, to show up with greetings from the newsroom.

Our coworkers had taken up a collection and gotten us a gift certificate at a local garden center so we could buy a tree to plant in Mike's memory, a pound of fine chocolate, and a couple's massage.

"We didn't know what would be appropriate," John said. "I know there's nothing that will make it better."

We sat out on the deck and ate chili and drank beer for hours, talking about work, about Mike, and about my plans.

The later it got, the more profane our jokes became. We finished all the beer and then the wine.

"Hey, didn't Coutlakis give you some scotch?" Boyle asked.

"Yes he did and it's put away."

We switched to coffee for a couple hours.

On April 10, Mike got his first disability check. A bulk check would follow in a few weeks. It had been thirty-seven months since he first applied. He was turned down twice despite having stage 3 cancer, and then he had to wait for a hearing, which was scheduled about six weeks before he died.

#

During the Bush administration, the number of people working in disability courts had been allowed to decline to about half of its previous level. In some districts, one or two judges handled the work of six or more. The average wait was thirty-six months where we live.

I would return to work on Wednesday, two weeks and a day after Mike died. I wanted to finish up all the paperwork before then, so I went back to the Register of Deeds office on Monday.

"It's not here yet," the woman behind the counter said when I asked for Mike's death certificate. This was the third time I had been in to try and get it, and it should have been ready by now.

"Well, what do I do?" I asked. "I need it."

"It's not here," she repeated and started to turn away.

I'd had enough.

"Look, isn't it enough that my kid is dead?" I asked loudly. "You know more about this stuff than I do. I've never lost a child before. What the hell do I know about how to get a death certificate?"

I wasn't yelling, but there was a note of panic in my voice, I'm sure. I had to send off copies to various agencies—and to the cable company—and I had hoped to have it all done before I went back to work.

Someone else came over and offered to help. She took my phone number and assured me that she would find out what happened by the end of the day. In fact, she did, and I had the death certificate in hand by five o'clock.

The death certificate wasn't my only frustration during those first weeks after Mike died. Christian had sent me Mike's medical records. As I read through them, I discovered his doctors had written that he needed a colonoscopy but couldn't afford it. Christian told me the doctor demanded $2,300 cash up front and there was no way Mike could have afforded it.

"Why didn't he ask me?" I asked.

"He knew you'd go into debt to pay for it and he didn't want that," Christian said.

Even more shocking was the record of the colonoscopy the doctor agreed to do three weeks before Mike first was hospitalized.

"...Unable to finish procedure. Next time use (pediatric) scope."

Mike's colon had been completely blocked and the doctor didn't even tell him. He sent him home, knowing he had a life-threatening condition.

I decided to call the hospital's ethicist to see whether Memorial Health System had a policy on doctors withholding knowledge of a life-threatening condition.

The first time I called, she was out, so I left a message. When she didn't call back in a few days, I called again. She was unavailable, so I left another message. I continued to leave messages for several days until finally, her administrative assistant e-mailed me with a time I could call.

I called at the designated time, and again, she was out.

So I called the hospital CEO and detailed my problems getting in touch with the ethicist.

"Look, I'm not going to sue you, but I think I am owed an apology for the way my son was treated," I told him. "I want to know the hospital's policy on its doctors withholding knowledge of a life-threatening condition, and I can't even get your ethicist to call me back."

She called that afternoon, full of apologies for missing my calls, and she agreed to take a look at Mike's records.

We e-mailed back and forth about what kind of an apology I wanted. I wanted a statement that the hospital expects its physicians to inform patients of life-threatening conditions and an apology for the hospital nearly killing Mike three times in a single year. The doctor had withheld information a second time when Mike developed the infection in the incision from his second surgery. Either that or Dr. Hammen was incompetent for not diagnosing the infection.

The ethicist finally decided I was asking for too much. I told her if I didn't get a written apology, I would be back in Savannah within six months, holding a photo of my dead son and telling the TV stations how he died.

She dismissed me with a snort that was more like a subdued giggle.

Four months later, we held our first Health Care for All Rally in Savannah and three television stations came to the event. One did an in-depth story the night before the event and then came that day to cover it.

I never got my apology, which leads me to believe that no one there cared that they sacrificed a human life. I wonder how many others have died needlessly at their hands.

James came to visit the weekend before I went back to work. I was planting the cherry tree we had bought in the backyard.

"I know this sounds a little nuts, but has Mike come to—you know—visit you?" he asked.

"No. Has he been to see you?"

"Well, I've had this dream a couple of times—really vivid. We're sitting on the couch, shooting the shit and somebody walks in. I say, 'Look who's here. It's Mike!' and the other person says, 'I thought he was dead.' Then he flashes me that big grin of his and says, 'I am dead, but I'm always here if you need me.'"

It was the same dream I had about Ellen. To me, this just confirmed that they were together because James had no way of knowing about my Ellen dream. I had never told Mike about it.

By Wednesday, I was ready to go back to work. I couldn't concentrate on anything, but I didn't want to sit at home and dwell on Mike's death, either.

Bruce had promised me light duty if I wanted it.

But when I got into the office, I found an e-mail with the stories of three young men with mental illnesses who had died after being released from state psychiatric hospitals, all within a couple of months. None had been given a discharge plan.

I needed to write this story. No person should die of neglect and I wanted people to know how frequently it happened.

I wondered whether I could be objective, but I decided if the state had a reasonable explanation as to why procedures had been ignored three times in as many months, I was willing to listen and to report on it.

Of course, there was no reasonable explanation. State hospitals were understaffed and overwhelmed. Nurses and other staff were working extra shifts; some even were forced to work double shifts. There just weren't enough people to get everything done the way it should be.

When I called the parents of the young men, one of the mothers told me I'd never understand unless I lost a child to medical neglect. I told her my son had just died from that very thing.

She opened up.

One of the three men had been dropped off at a homeless shelter that had been closed for several months. He was placed in a hotel, where he died three weeks later from a drug overdose.

The other two died from suicide.

All three deaths were unnecessary, and because the parents had been willing to speak openly about their sons' mental illnesses, readers were able to see how tragic their lives and deaths really were.

As soon as the story ran, the state changed its policy to require discharge plans for every patient at every state hospital.

Of course, the hospitals were still understaffed and horror stories abounded. When I could get verification, I told the stories.

But telling the stories didn't seem to make much difference. The state continued to underfund its mental health and substance abuse programs, and people continued to fall through the cracks.

Occasionally, as with the story on these deaths, I was able to get the state to tweak its policy, but I knew that until society changed its mind on the worth of every human life, no real change could come.

On Bruce's advice, I didn't write stories about people trying to raise money for cancer treatment because it was too close to home. Those stories were given to other reporters.

I was still having trouble concentrating. Some days I couldn't read my e-mails. I felt as though I was being dragged back to the moment of Mike's death several times a day. It was immobilizing.

A hospice grief counselor likened it to walking along the beach and being slammed by a huge wave.

"You get up and walk on," she said. "It will happen again and again, but it will be less and less often."

I dropped out of the church choir because I had lost my love of singing. I was always tired. I wasn't even reading anymore, which was what used to help me go to sleep at night. I picked up a book or a magazine and read the same passage over and over again. I wanted to cry but I couldn't. I didn't want to be here, but I didn't want to die by my own hand either.

I was fortunate in having friends who didn't mind if I talked about Mike. If they grew tired of hearing about him, they never said anything to me about it. No one told me to move on, get over it, or start enjoying life again.

In fact, people were surprisingly sensitive. No one told me he was with Jesus or that it was God's will or that the Lord moves in mysterious ways. My friends simply hugged me or listened or laughed or cried with me.

Liz, the friend who had spent Mike's final Thanksgiving with us, knew she could always get a laugh out of me by saying that Mike had come to her in a dream and told her he wanted her to have the face jug, and she has done so again and again. I never tire of it.

"It's so vivid," she says. "He's coming to me and telling me the jug is meant for me. I have to come over and get it."

I can see the dream. Mike is holding the jug out to her and smiling. And the jug stays with me anyway.

Chapter 29

Six weeks after Mike died, Shannon graduated from her RN program, with honors. I drove out to Fayetteville for the graduation and KJ flew in from Massachusetts. Matt had just gotten back from deployment in Qatar.

We toasted Ellen with a pot of coffee and Bailey's Irish Crème, and we toasted Mike with coffee sans alcohol.

As Shannon sat in a crowd of one thousand graduates, I couldn't help but see how much she looked like Ellen, and to know how proud Ellen would have been. She graduated with honors despite having two small children and a husband deployed to the Middle East. She was six hundred miles from most of her family, three hundred from me.

On my way home from Fayetteville, I stopped in Raleigh to see Janet. We started talking about how many horror stories must be out there and wondered how many people died the way Mike did.

The answer would be triple the fifteen to seventeen thousand a year we estimated after doing a search for information. But those were the numbers I used when talking to people about the need for universal access to health care.

I remembered my friend Bill Jamieson's belief that telling stories is what makes a difference. Putting faces on public policy is what I had been doing for a quarter century but I hadn't been able to stop the death of my child.

So, how could we gather stories and make people see that human beings were suffering and dying? Most people I talked to had no idea that the emergency room was inadequate as a fallback for a permanent medical home. Mike had gone there three times and gotten laxatives and pain meds for a cancerous tumor blocking his colon.

I wasn't very tech-savvy at the time, but Janet was a freelance web designer (she had been fired from her job because she took too much time off when Mike died), and she suggested we put up a website and solicit stories.

We called it Life o' Mike (later, as our work expanded, we changed the name to Western North Carolina Health Advocates, on the web as www.wnchealthadvocates.org). I started by telling his story, and I would blog about my journey through this experience of losing a child to a broken system.

I hoped to collect stories and maybe gather signatures for a petition asking the next president to expand access to health care. I knew I wanted to talk to legislators about how people were dying, but most of all, I wanted to educate people who held the power of the vote.

Janet would design the website and show me how to use it. If something I wanted to do was beyond my then-limited ability, she would either teach me how to do it or take care of it herself.

We decided the theme should be plaid, since that was Mike's "favorite color." Four years later, a consultant would try to get me to change the theme to a solid color, but after speaking to board members and volunteers, he relented.

"Whenever I see plaid, I think of Mike and how he died and how much I want things to change," one board member told the consultant.

I left Janet a CD of all the photos we had used in the slide show at Mike's memorial service, and she started designing our first website.

I got home late in the day, and as I often do in the spring, I decided to walk around the house to see what was sprouting and blooming. We had a couple of rose bushes outside the window of Mike's room that had never bloomed. I was planning to dig them up, but as I got out of the car and looked up at the house, the bushes were covered in beautiful, deep red blooms—dozens of them. I took it as a message from Mike that he was OK and I was on the right track.

The roses have bloomed every year since.

I continued to write about social justice issues at work, and things continued to not change, so I decided holding rallies was the next step.

I went to the publisher and he gave me approval to hold rallies as long as I didn't put forth any specific plan and didn't use the paper's name to promote events. The paper would list the rallies in its events section, but would not mention my name.

We opened that first rally in Savannah with the song, "Always Look on the Bright Side of Life," and we encouraged people to tell their stories. One woman spoke about losing her job when she became ill, and with the job went her insurance. She was destitute and deep in debt—and still sick.

Danny, who is very shy, took the microphone and wondered whether Congress might act if the emergency room became their only hope for access to care.

Trey, who was just six, asked to speak. He held the microphone for a full minute before he finally took a deep breath and choked out, "I miss my Uncle Mike."

He handed back the microphone and went over to sit in Jennifer's lap and cried uncontrollably for fifteen minutes. Jennifer's shirt was wet from his tears when he finally sat up and dried his eyes.

Uncle Mike was the one person who could be as silly as Trey. He was going to teach Trey to play guitar. It was a huge loss and Trey didn't know how to deal with it.

The rally wasn't huge—only about fifty people – but it was enough to encourage me to continue.

Before the first rally, we went on our annual summer trip to visit friends and family in New Jersey and New England. We brought Peyton with us, pretty much because she asked to come.

On a hike in eastern Pennsylvania, Bruce and Craig McKeown started talking politics. Barack Obama had won the Democratic nomination and Craig, a Hillary Clinton supporter, was disappointed. They started to talk about a rumor that Michelle Obama had called Clinton a "honky."

That was when I lost my cool. I stopped and turned around and blasted both of them.

"People are dying because of disastrous public policy. You knew one of them—watched him grow up, be refused needed medical care, and die, and you're talking about whether the wife of one candidate called another candidate a bad name. If you can't talk about policy, don't talk about politics. I'm tired of people looking at what Mike always called the shiny crap and not at the issues."

I turned back around and started walking again. I turned my attention to Peyton, who had developed a blister on her heel. I didn't want to discuss this brand of politics anymore.

I had called in to a talk radio show three weeks after Mike died to say the same thing. I listened regularly to the Stephanie Miller show because she's funny. This one morning, callers were talking about whether Obama should wear a flag pin on his lapel. The more they talked about it, the angrier I got. So I went outside, sat on a bench on the sidewalk, and dialed the number. The screener told me to hold on and Stephanie would be with me. Five minutes later, I was on the air.

"Three weeks ago, my son died because our health care system is completely broken," I said. "He was denied care and allowed to get so sick we could have brought criminal charges if they continued to do nothing. But it was too late to save him. He's not alone. People are dying every day because our health care system is so broken. I don't give a damn whether Barack Obama wears a flag pinned to his lapel. What I care about is whether he will work to fix this. That's what it will take to get my vote, not whether he wears a cheap lapel pin."

Stephanie agreed with me.

I got calls from friends who had heard me, thanking me for speaking out.

I would continue to speak out, not just on a call-in radio show, but at rallies and to legislators and policy makers, at press conferences and on television.

Our second rally was in Asheville in October. Christina flew in from Massachusetts, Shannon came from Fayetteville, and Danny and family came from Georgia. Janet and James came from Raleigh and about two hundred people from around Asheville came to hear the facts about why we needed health reform.

I made it clear that this wasn't a political rally. We weren't there to talk about the merits of one candidate over another; we were there to talk about demanding our broken health care system be fixed. I also made it clear that we should be open to solutions and not think we had the only workable ideas.

"The point is to get people talking like adults," I said. "We can do this because this is America and we can do anything we set our minds to."

Members of the local Tea Party were not happy about my speaking out. Almost immediately, they started making noises about how I should be fired because I was biased.

But I never advocated for any one solution; I only said people were dying and that we as a nation should do something about it.

The battle would get worse as time went on, and the Tea Party demanded that I tell their "side" of the story, which was that people could go to the emergency room for care, or that the "free market" should be allowed to handle it.

But my son died because the free market didn't force insurance companies to sell to people who had pre-existing conditions. The free market also allowed lifetime caps on coverage so that one little girl I wrote about had surpassed the cap before her first birthday because she had needed a heart transplant.

And I was writing stories about the number of people who had lost insurance in the previous couple of years in North Carolina because so many jobs had moved overseas and factories across the state had closed.

After one such story, I got a call from the Heritage Foundation asking if I would quote their expert in my next story. I asked for information on their expert and I received an e-mail with a quote from a woman who said we needed to take away ALL regulation from the insurance companies and allow the market to fix the mess.

I replied saying that if I quoted their expert I also would have to quote someone who would debunk it with real research and real numbers. The woman called me again and said she would complain to my editor.

"You must be one of those people who claim that innocent people are dying when all they need to do is get a job with insurance or buy a policy," she said.

"Yes, people are dying," I said. "We need an honest conversation about how to fix this, not false rhetoric."

"Right. Name one person you know who died."

"My son."

Dead silence for about ten seconds, then, "I'm sorry to have brought that to the surface."

"You didn't. It already lives there."

I explained that my son had been unable to buy insurance at any price, and employers' insurance was likely to demand a rider or refuse to cover anything related to his birth defect, and that was because the unregulated market allowed it to happen that way.

She never called again, never demanded that I quote her expert, never called me biased, and never called my editor.

It isn't biased to know when something is broken. It isn't biased to report on the fact that more and more people were losing insurance coverage.

I was being asked to speak publically about Mike's death more often, and I began to think about trying to turn the website into a nonprofit. Getting incorporated was easy, but I dreaded the forms I would have to fill out for our 501 (c) (3) tax-exempt status.

Chapter 30

As I thought about making Life o' Mike a nonprofit so I could solicit tax-deductible donations, I knew I needed to raise money to make it happen. A friend gave me money to get the ball rolling with T-shirts.

We ordered black shirts emblazoned with "HEALTH CARE FOR ALL" and our website name, and plaid magnetic "ribbons" with the same slogan.

We had a couple hundred dollars when Chat Norvell, president of the CarePartners Foundation, invited me to lunch to offer his help in getting my work off the ground.

"Well, I could use more money to buy T-shirts to sell," I said.

He wanted to do something more, he said. He offered to pay for an attorney to help me get my tax-free status as a nonprofit.

I hadn't expected such a generous gift and I was relieved beyond measure to be able to have someone else fill out and file the forms. We had our 501(c)(3) status in less than four months, thanks to attorney Eileen McMinn, who later sat for three years on the board of Life o' Mike's successor, Western North Carolina Health Advocates.

I was still under the impression that funding would come easily and I would be able to go full-time soon.

About fifteen months after Mike died, I went to work full-time at the nonprofit, but it wasn't because of funding.

I had been speaking about the lack of access to care for an increasing number of Americans. The number of uninsured had risen from 16 million when I first started writing about the health care crisis in 1992 to 45 million in 2009.

I was still writing the same stories about people who were trying to raise money to get care. Those who were fortunate to get into the newspaper often raised thousands of dollars, although that wasn't necessarily enough to pay for treatment, since chemotherapy averages about $250,000 per round.

I was speaking to groups about these statistics and asking people to think about solutions and to let their legislators know that we expected them to come up with some public policy that would allow people to get access to care.

Tea Party members were watching and waiting for me to say something about single-payer, but I was careful to avoid it. I was speaking as a person who had seen what lack of access to care could do, not as a newspaper reporter who had covered the mess.

I was careful to ask groups to list my affiliation with Life o' Mike and not mention the newspaper, since I had received permission to speak under those terms.

Then in July, a group listed me as "reporter for the *Citizen-Times*" on a poster, and the Tea Party pounced.

I canceled the talk. The executive editor instructed me to take down the Life o' Mike website and told me that he would have to approve every blog post when it went back up.

I went to the publisher, knowing I would have to resign. He made it clear he wanted me to stay at the paper.

"People know you give fair coverage of the issues," he said. "You shouldn't let these haters end your newspaper career."

But Phil, the editor, wanted the authority to approve or deny my personal blog posts, and I couldn't allow that. Phil was timid when it came to offending the Tea Party, and I was certain no post would be safe enough for his approval.

I knew I had to leave, but I agreed to sleep on it.

I called Rob, who liked the idea of me sleeping on it, but then he called back five minutes later and said, "I think we should just say fuck it and go for what's right. Let's have dinner out to celebrate your new career."

I went in and told the publisher I was leaving.

"What will you do for income?" he asked.

I didn't know, but I knew I had to leave.

"Can you wait two weeks?"

Well, I had planned on giving two weeks' notice, but he had something else in mind. The company was planning layoffs in the newsroom in a couple of weeks and I could volunteer to go that way.

"You'll get a severance package and unemployment compensation," he said. "But you can't tell anyone until the layoffs are announced."

So, I volunteered to be laid off, and another reporter who would have lost her job stepped into my position.

Meanwhile, the Tea Party inundated me, my editor, and the publisher with vicious e-mails. One told me she didn't care that my son had died and that I should be fired.

One of the leaders of the Tea Party wanted to come in and talk to the publisher about me. She arrived with a cameraman, and the publisher informed her he wouldn't discuss any personnel issues with her, with or without the camera, and that he wouldn't discuss anything with the camera. He escorted her from the building.

The right-wing blogosphere in Buncombe County was up in arms over the "injustice" of my continuing to have a job. They reportedly tried to get *Fox News* to come do a story on me.

I sat quietly in the newsroom, editing copy and waiting for my liberation. I had promised a friend of mine who writes the popular blog, Ashevegas, that I would make a statement to him if he would refrain from writing what the right-wingers were saying until I could speak.

Danny, whose personality requires that everything be planned, thought I was nuts to leave a thirty-year career for the uncertainty of advocacy work.

"What will you do?" he asked, panic rising in his voice.

"I'll advocate for health care for everyone so people will stop dying the way your brother did," I said.

He took it on himself to call one of the most vocal of the Tea Party people.

"Don't you realize how bad it looks for people to think you forced a bereaved mother from her job?" he asked.

"We're going to silence her," the man replied.

"No you won't! You're handing her a microphone," Danny said. "She's free to speak her mind, which she hasn't done in public yet. She's going to be everywhere talking about my brother's death. You don't know her."

So the man offered to beat up Danny. My son is a former Marine and he's still in pretty good shape. The next time Danny came to visit, he asked if we could go to the video store where the man worked to pick out a movie to watch.

"I promise not to start anything," he said, chuckling.

We didn't go.

But he did arrange a meeting with the woman who led the Buncombe County Tea Party. She had a son with a serious chronic illness, and I couldn't understand what she thought was going to happen when he aged out of her health insurance.

She was cordial, and her son and my grandson played well together for a couple hours.

As a reporter, I had to learn to get along with people who stood for everything I disagreed with. I learned that you can still respect—and even like—someone whose views are a polar opposite to your own. The lessons learned as a reporter would serve me well in the coming battle for health reform.

I know how to let people disagree with me without getting angry about it. I can be respectful and still disagree. I walk away from name calling and nastiness because I know that person isn't going to listen to what I have to say, and I've already heard all the talking points opponents of reform have to offer.

If someone is open to talking respectfully, I'm happy to have the conversation, whether we agree or not.

I made appointments with legislators at the state and federal levels to talk about how we might fix the system. By this time, President Obama was in office and working on the Affordable Care Act. Already, some were claiming he was moving too fast.

But most Americans didn't have all the information about just how broken the system was. The *Journal of the American Medical Association* published a study by Harvard Medical School that calculated the number of Americans who were dying from lack of access to health care. Their estimate came to forty-five thousand a year—one every twelve minutes.

I called the paper to ask whether there would be a story on this and I was told, "Only if the AP moves a story." Translation: If the Associated Press didn't write a story about it, most papers weren't going to have a story, and few Americans would know about these devastating losses.

The next morning I looked through the newspaper and found nothing. I went to the websites of several major newspapers and searched and found nothing. I looked for a couple hours and found stories in only two newspapers: The *Boston Globe* and the *Sacramento Bee*.

I sat down and wrote an op-ed piece about the findings and the major media's lack of coverage. It ran several days later.

My take was that an American was dying once every twelve minutes, and there was no such problem as moving too fast. Opponents of reform, most of whom called themselves "pro-life," didn't seem to be overly concerned about the lives that were already born, just the "preborn."

I sat down with my member of congress, Heath Shuler, and explained it to him.

"You can't be pro-life if your support for life stops at the end of the birth canal," I said.

He assured me he was for giving care to veterans, children, and the elderly, and I told him that wasn't enough. It was easy for him, a multi-millionaire with the best health benefits available anywhere to pretend nothing could happen to him or his family, I said. I went on to say that I hoped he never had to endure what my family has been through.

I had two rallies in Asheville, which drew about three hundred to four hundred people and were covered by local media. I tried to arrange a rally in Raleigh on the State House lawn, but the state made a mess of the paperwork and when I arrived to set up, I found police lines and orange cones everywhere. An officer asked what I was doing there, so I showed him the paperwork.

He hadn't heard about it. Someone had forgotten to enter our rally into the calendar. We were fine to go ahead and hold the rally.

The problem was that the state had approved a protest by the Westboro Baptist Church right next to where we were scheduled to be. People who wanted to come to our rally saw and heard Westboro's hatred and vitriol and left. We had about a dozen people.

Janet had a little fun with the protesters as we were leaving, telling them she loved gays. I told them God loves everyone—even them. Of course, they spewed hatred at us. Finally a state police officer asked us not to incite them anymore because, as amusing as it was, he didn't trust them not to become violent.

I would go back to Raleigh for many protests. I would even be arrested for trying to speak to legislators about health care. But I never tried to organize another rally of my own there.

At home, I approached my pastor to ask if we could have a memorial service at our church for all the people who have died. He was eager to help put it together.

We invited people from a variety of faiths to talk about the immorality of allowing a person to die every twelve minutes rather than change the policy that allowed it. We also asked people who needed insurance or care and couldn't get it to come and speak.

Each person had twelve minutes to speak, and at the end of the twelve minutes, we chimed a Tibetan brass bowl to remind people that an American had died from lack of access to health care.

My pastor was on the board of the state Council of Churches, which invited me to Raleigh for a similar service. Within a few weeks I was invited to Washington, DC, by the National Council of Churches for an outdoor memorial service for the people who were dying from lack of medical care.

Each time I told Mike's story, it took a little out of me, and I was telling it frequently, to groups and to individuals. When I spoke in Washington, I lost it and wept when I said how much I miss my son every minute of every day.

Senator Bernie Sanders, who had walked over from the Senate Chamber, stepped over and hugged me after I spoke. He promised he would continue to work for reform. Beside him was Representative Sheila Jackson Lee, who also hugged me and promised to work for reform.

"Your son's story is so compelling," she told me. "Keep telling it. People can deny many things, but they can't deny a true story."

Chapter 31

I was starting to speak at more gatherings—I was a keynote speaker at the Martin Luther King Day event in Asheville in 2010, and at the annual fundraising dinner of a free clinic in Waynesville, a half hour west of Asheville.

At the dinner, I spoke about the need for places where people could get care. I talked about Mike's illness and death, and I noticed some of the burly men in the audience were daubing at their eyes. The clinic director told me afterward that most of the people in the audience were conservatives, and that I had changed a few minds about the need for access to care for everyone.

"When people hear a story like yours, they see the need to fix the system," she said. "Keep telling it."

In late 2009, I was invited to go to Washington with Health Care for America Now, to tell Mike's story. I joined about twenty-five other activists, including the eleven-year-old boy who stood next to president Obama as he signed the Affordable Care Act into law.

Susan Braig, an artist, was another of the people in attendance. She had taken out a catastrophic health plan—just in case—and had developed breast cancer. Because it was a catastrophic plan with a lot of small print, she discovered the policy didn't cover chemotherapy if it was outpatient, and it didn't cover the anti-nausea medications she needed.

"I realized that I was paying more for medications than I would to buy precious gemstones," she said.

That's when she decided to make jewelry out of expired drugs. Viagra looks like turquoise; Coricidin looks like red coral. So she made a necklace and earrings and called the set, "Well Hung."

Kelly Cuvar had cancer that hadn't once been in remission in thirteen years, and she was having problems accessing the care she needed, even though she was covered by Medicaid.

Heather Mroz was a young mother of twins born two months early. She was buried in debt because her insurance company had canceled her policy when she was six months pregnant and starting to have contractions. Her debt ran to almost half a million dollars.

Another young man had gone blind because he couldn't afford the surgery that would have saved his sight.

We were trained to tell our stories in under two minutes (which I already had down), and in nonviolent resistance, and then went out to demonstrate in front of the US Chamber of Commerce Building. The Chamber had been chosen because of its lobbying efforts at preventing the Affordable Care Act from passing.

We made the evening news. We educated some people but that was about the extent of our impact that day.

#

In February of 2010, the push for passage of the ACA was at its peak, as was the resistance to it. Those in opposition were spending millions every day to buy votes against it, and we were a grassroots movement.

We met again in Washington, this time to help stage a huge rally and demonstration outside the Ritz Carlton, where insurance industry executives were meeting.

I was one of those willing to be arrested for refusing to clear away from the front door of the hotel, if it came to that. I was also scheduled to be on the Ed Shultz television show the second night of my stay.

We were placed at the head of the march—about five thousand people—as it worked its way toward a park for the beginning of the rally. Howard Dean was the featured speaker, and as we reached the podium, he asked me to tell him about the photo I was carrying.

"This is my son, Mike," I said. "He died because a birth defect is a pre-existing condition so he couldn't get insurance, and without it, he was denied the care he needed until it was too late to save his life."

"May I borrow the picture? I promise to give it back."

Dean is a physician. He knows what happens when people can't get the care they need. He was a strong advocate of the Affordable Care Act, although he wanted a so-called public option, which would allow people to buy into a single-payer system instead of relying entirely on the private insurance industry. Since it is exempt from antitrust laws, the insurance industry has an effective monopoly, and without the public option, people really had no choice other than which part of the monopoly would get their business.

"Big insurance is in the Ritz Carlton right now, trying to figure out how to derail any law that would regulate them," Dean said. "They're trying to figure out how not to cover you, and here's what happens when you can't get coverage," he continued as he held Mike's picture high.

"This is Mike. He died because Big Insurance didn't have to sell him coverage . . . So, who do we stand with today, Big Insurance or Mike?"

The crowd began to chant: "Mike, Mike, Mike . . ."

All I could think of was how much Mike loved to be the center of attention and how much he would have loved this. I could almost hear his voice, chanting "Me, me, me!" followed by his maniacal laugh.

I had to steady myself to stay on my feet. I missed him so much. But I was doing what he asked. I was trying my best to be positive. I hadn't sued anyone, nor would I.

After Howard Dean finished, we moved on to the street in front of the Ritz Carlton. A reporter from *ABC World News Tonight* had seen Mike's picture in the park and wanted to interview me. I never saw the footage, but a number of people saw it and told me I had done a good job.

I worked my way over to the entrance of the Ritz Carlton in time to hear a police officer tell us we wouldn't be arrested.

"Why not?" someone asked.

"Look, we're on your side," he said. "They're coming after our benefits soon. We know we're next."

We talked them into escorting a dozen or so of us from the front door and through the parking garage to the next block.

An older officer took me by the arm. "Thank you for what you're doing," he said. "People need to know."

It turned out his best friend's granddaughter had died after she was in an auto accident and was sent home by doctors in the emergency room. She died in her sleep that night from a lack of insurance.

We called ourselves the Ritz Carlton 14 and laughed as we walked back to the rally in time to hear NAACP President Ben Jealous speak from the back of a flatbed truck.

Susan Braig and I got back to the hotel room, eager to tune in and see our protest on the news.

On CNN, Rick Sanchez showed footage of the demonstration, clearly thousands of people crammed into a block.

"*Dozens* of people gathered to protest—and you're not going to believe this—they were demonstrating *in favor* of Obamacare!"

Susan and I were incredulous. How could anyone look at that footage and say "dozens" of people. It was obvious there were thousands of people.

We turned off the news.

The next day, some of us would speak before an informal Congressional hearing, telling our stories of denial of care, inadequate care and the resulting pain and suffering.

I was asked to do my chiming bowl thing once again. No matter what was happening, I stood up every twelve minutes and chimed the brass bowl that the people from Health Care for America Now had run out and bought for me when I mentioned the memorial service I had done earlier.

That bowl sits on my desk now to remind me that even though the death toll is lower, we still have work to do.

The first time I chimed, several photographers approached and asked if I would chime again so they could get a shot. I told them I would—in eleven minutes.

Talk show host Ed Shultz was in the audience and as Heather told her story, he began to tear up. By the time Heather was finished, he was sobbing. He asked Heather to join me on his show that night.

Also at the hearing was Wendell Potter, a former vice president for one of the huge insurance companies. Potter had left the insurance industry and become a whistle-blower. He had appeared on a number of national programs to talk about the necessity of health reform.

I was planning to visit my congressman, Heath Shuler, a Blue Dog Democrat who hadn't said whether he would support the Affordable Care Act.

Shuler knew me. I had spoken to him a number of times about the need for access to care for people from ages eighteen to sixty-four. He was fond of bragging that we were taking care of children, veterans, and our elders, and I was fond of telling him forty-five thousand Americans were dying every year because we weren't taking care of them.

I had made an appointment, and Wendell Potter asked if he could accompany me. Regina Holliday, whose husband died of kidney cancer because of a lack of health insurance, also came along. She lives in Washington, DC, which has no representative in Congress.

Regina is an artist who painted murals of her husband's final days and gained the attention of the national media.

Shuler's receptionist told us he was out, but when someone opened an office door, I saw him standing behind it. "Oh good, he's in," I said.

We were ushered in and I asked Shuler whether he was pro-life.

"Of course I am," he said.

I told him any definition of pro-life has to include that stretch between birth and death.

"You can't be pro-life if your support for life ends at the end of the birth canal," I said. "And if you vote against the Affordable Care Act, I will call you out on it."

He voted against the law.

In the fall of 2010, I was invited to take part in an activists' summit in Washington, DC, sponsored by Consumers Union. We heard from Elizabeth Warren and others who work toward a more just society. During a legislative luncheon, I had the chance to speak to Nancy Pelosi, who was still Speaker of the House.

I handed her a photo of Mike and thanked her for getting through what she could. The Affordable Care Act, as it was passed, probably would have saved Mike's life if it had been passed five years earlier.

Tears filled her eyes as she embraced me and told me she wished she could have done more.

Chapter 32

In 2012, I met Reverend Dr. William Barber II, the president of the NC NAACP and the architect of what would become known as the Moral Monday Movement.

Reverend Barber heard me speak at a gathering about poverty in August, and asked me to join the annual rally in Raleigh known as HKonJ (Historic Thousands on Jones Street, which is held in front of the NC General Assembly Building each February).

In October, to celebrate the first day of the insurance marketplaces, I was invited to speak at a press conference in Washington, DC. The government was shut down by Republicans intent on defunding the Affordable Care Act, but I stood between Nancy Pelosi and Senator Harry Reid and talked about how many lives this law had the potential to save.

By then it was clear that some GOP-dominated states would not expand Medicaid to care for all people in poverty, and that thousands would die as a result. As I clutched my son's photo, I vowed to stay in the fight until every human being has access to quality, affordable, health care.

"I'm not afraid of anything you might do to me as I fight for this," I said, raising Mike's picture in the air. "The most precious thing anyone can have has been taken from me already, so I fear nothing."

Our state legislature changed hands in the 2012 election, and its leaders were refusing to meet with anyone who opposed their ultra-conservative actions. I spoke to a crowd of eight thousand to twelve thousand people, who roared approval at my view that legislators should stop calling themselves pro-life if their support for life ended at birth.

A few weeks later, a few dozen of us gathered again in Raleigh to compose letters to the new Speaker of the House,

Representative Thom Tillis. We had many different causes, since the HKonJ Coalition is made up of dozens of organizations and individuals, and each of us was ready to deliver a letter to Tillis about why legislation passed or being considered by the new legislative majority was ill-advised.

We walked from a nearby church to the General Assembly Building and Reverend Barber knelt to pray before we went in.

Barber walks with a cane because he has a rare form of arthritis. For a time, he couldn't walk at all. He believes his mobility is a miracle, and he is forever on the lookout for more miracles—including a change of heart in the legislature.

He walked into the front door of Tillis's office and a moment later, Tillis burst out the back door, purple with rage.

"Let's move!" he called to two aides, and then ran down the corridor away from us.

Barber walked out of the office and over to me. He leaned on his cane and shook his head.

"It looks like we'll have to so some direct action," he said.

"I'm there," I replied.

#

Six weeks later, on April 29, Barber and sixteen others entered the General Assembly Building to exercise their right under the NC State Constitution to address our legislators. They were arrested.

The next Monday, about thirty more people followed suit, and on May 13, forty-nine of us went in and stood outside the Senate and House Chamber doors. We chanted, sang, and prayed. I held Mike's picture high as we prayed for wisdom from within those chambers.

After a few minutes, Lieutenant Martin Brock of the General Assembly Police came through the crowd with a megaphone, telling us we had five minutes to clear the building or we would be arrested—or at least that's what I think he said. It was pretty loud in there as we exercised our right to be in that public building and speak.

Indeed, we were arrested, handcuffed, and brought downstairs to be processed before being loaded onto two prison buses.

Among those arrested were a reporter and an elderly Methodist minister named Vernon Tyson, a longtime civil rights activist. Neither was within the area specified by police, but they apparently were caught up in the fervor of the moment.

Once we were loaded onto the bus, Yara Allen began singing, "We Shall Not Be Moved." A tall African American man boarded the bus and let one of his hands slip out of his cuffs.

"I'm free," he mouthed, smiling.

"Are you crazy?" I asked. "Don't you realize how much trouble you could cause yourself?"

He slipped his hand back into the zip-tie and leaned into me.

"Lady, we already on a prison bus. How much worse do you think it's gonna get?"

The man was Reverend Barber's brother-in-law, Mike McLean, and we would become fast friends as I drove four hours each way, week after week, to participate in Moral Mondays and stay at the jailhouse until everyone was released, notarizing first-appearance waivers. Laurel Ashton, a young field secretary, also was arrested that night. Reverend Barber would come to court in our support as our cases, and Yara's, were tried together and we moved through the process of appearance after appearance before we were tried and convicted.

We later would have those convictions overturned.

When the governor claimed the arrestees were out-of-state agitators, my notary records proved less than 7 percent of those arrested were out-of-state people. The conservative organization, Civitas, also helped by posting every arrestee's mug shot, address, and personal information on its website. In trying to intimidate us, they proved we were not from outside of North Carolina and helped many of us contact each other to coordinate rides to our court dates in Raleigh.

Governor Pat McCrory then said he had come out to a Moral Monday rally and had been treated rudely. That, too, proved to be a lie.

The numbers kept rising, and by the time the 2013 legislative session ended, a thousand of us had been arrested. Later, nearly all of us would be acquitted because we were on public property exercising our rights when we were hauled off for trespassing, and the other charges of "chanting and loud singing" and "carrying signs" were found to be a violation of our free-speech rights.

Each week, the number of people attending the rallies increased. From a couple dozen people on April 29, to twelve thousand the final week of the 2013 rallies. Buses came from around the state, including from Asheville, where I live. I continued to make the four-hour drive on my own, with one or two friends to keep me company, because I attended the pre-rally meetings at a nearby church, and I would stay after the rally until everyone was out of jail. A couple of times that meant a twenty-hour day, but it was worth being part of this historic movement.

I spoke at the rallies when the focus was on health care, and I was part of the security team other weeks. When HKonJ rolled around again, I was asked to speak.

I gazed out at a sea of people. Five city blocks, packed solid, rooftops full, and people crowded onto side streets. The police had told us that fifteen to twenty thousand people could fit into each city block, making the crowd number between eighty and one hundred thousand people. I had never seen so many people in one place, and I had two minutes to make my case.

I called out legislators who refused to expand Medicaid and again said that to be pro-life they had to actually support life.

"The blood of those who will die the way my son did is on your hands," I said.

I needed people to understand that five to seven people are dying every day in North Carolina, that five to seven families are enduring the pain of losing someone they love unnecessarily and that we can—and must—change this.

"I will not go away," I vowed. "I will fight until every human being has access to care. I am in this fight! You'll carry me out feet first! I hope y'all are with me."

I stepped away from the microphone, tears welling in my eyes, to the deafening noise as people cheered for the right of all people to have access to health care.

This isn't about me; it never has been. This is about saving lives. No one should die the way my precious son did.

The fight isn't over, and it won't be until every human being has access to the care they need. Health care is not a privilege, nor is it a commodity; it is a basic human right.

I can't get my son back, but I can work to save other people's children, brothers, sisters, aunts, uncles, and friends.

If you want to say every life matters, you need to believe it. You need to work for it. You need to live it.

CPSIA information can be obtained
at www.ICGtesting.com
Printed in the USA
LVOW01s0459010216
473132LV00023B/585/P

9 781944 680091